Third Eye

Your Guide to Third Eye Awakening and Psychic Development

© **Copyright 2020**

This document is geared towards providing exact and reliable information in regard to the topic and issue covered. The publication is sold with the idea that the publisher is not required to render accounting, officially permitted, or otherwise, qualified services. If advice is necessary, legal or professional, a practiced individual in the profession should be ordered.

- From a Declaration of Principles which was accepted and approved equally by a Committee of the American Bar Association and a Committee of Publishers and Associations.

In no way is it legal to reproduce, duplicate, or transmit any part of this document in either electronic means or in printed format. Recording of this publication is strictly prohibited and any storage of this document is not allowed unless with written permission from the publisher. All rights reserved.

The information provided herein is stated to be truthful and consistent, in that any liability, in terms of inattention or otherwise, by any usage or abuse of any policies, processes, or directions contained within is the solitary and utter responsibility of the recipient reader. Under no circumstances will any legal responsibility or blame be held against the publisher for any reparation, damages, or monetary loss due to the information herein, either directly or indirectly.

Respective authors own all copyrights not held by the publisher.

The information herein is offered for informational purposes solely, and is universal as so. The presentation of the information is without contract or any type of guarantee assurance.

The trademarks that are used are without any consent, and the publication of the trademark is without permission or backing by the trademark owner. All trademarks and brands within this book are for clarifying purposes only and are the owned by the owners themselves, not affiliated with this document.

Your Free Gift (only available for a limited time)

Thanks for getting this book! If you want to learn more about various spirituality topics, then join Mari Silva's community and get a free guided meditation MP3 for awakening your third eye. This guided meditation mp3 is designed to open and strengthen ones third eye so you can experience a higher state of consciousness. Simply visit the link below the image to get started.

https://spiritualityspot.com/meditation

Contents

PART 1: THIRD EYE AWAKENING 0
INTRODUCTION 1
CHAPTER ONE: UNDERSTANDING THE THIRD EYE CHAKRA 7
CHAPTER TWO: THE PINEAL GLAND: THE SCIENCE BEHIND THE THIRD EYE CHAKRA 15
CHAPTER THREE: LAYING THE GROUNDWORK: EXERCISES FOR OPENING THE THIRD EYE 25
CHAPTER FOUR: MEDITATION: THE CORNERSTONE OF THIRD EYE AWAKENING 42
CHAPTER FIVE: THE THIRD EYE CHAKRA AND EVERYDAY LIFE: HOW TO NOURISH YOUR THIRD EYE 51
CHAPTER SIX: BALANCING THE SEVEN CHAKRAS 63
CHAPTER SEVEN: HOW TO READ AURAS 74
CHAPTER EIGHT: PSYCHIC VISIONS AND CLAIRVOYANCE 89
CHAPTER NINE: GENERAL TIPS AND RECOMMENDATIONS 97
CHAPTER TEN: PUTTING IT ALL TOGETHER 107
CONCLUSION 116
PART 2: PSYCHIC 117
INTRODUCTION 118
CHAPTER 1: THE PSYCHIC: WHAT DOES IT MEAN TO BE PSYCHIC? 120
CHAPTER 2: MEDITATION: THE FIRST STEP 129

CHAPTER 3: INTUITION 140

CHAPTER 4: THE CLAIRS: CLAIRVOYANCE, CLAIRAUDIENCE, CLAIRGUSTANCE, CLAIRCOGNIZANCE AND CLAIRSENTIENCE .. 151

CHAPTER 5: TELEPATHY 163

CHAPTER 6: MEDIUMSHIP 172

CHAPTER 7: PSYCHOMETRY 181

CHAPTER 8: AURA READING 188

CHAPTER 9: HEALING 199

CHAPTER 10: CONTACTING AND COMMUNICATING WITH YOUR SPIRIT GUIDES 206

CONCLUSION 216

REFERENCES 218

Part 1: Third Eye Awakening

An Essential Guide to Opening Your Third Eye Chakra and Experiencing Higher Consciousness, Psychic Visions and Clairvoyance along with Tips for Balancing Chakras and Seeing Auras

Introduction

There is an untapped goldmine that exists within each and every one of us, a tremendous treasure trove that defies imagination. Those who choose to tap into it undergo an amazing and lifelong transformation. This unique class of people comes to realize that deep wisdom, mental and emotional wellbeing, and enduring happiness are not attainable through the external world but through an internal force that resides within us. This is the force of the energy centers known as chakras and, specifically, the third eye chakra.

In order to unleash this internal energy, we must awaken and empower the third eye chakra, also called "the eye of wisdom," the "mind's eye" or the "inner eye." In the majority of people, the third eye is dormant and remains dormant throughout their lives unless they voluntarily take steps to open it.

Once you have learned how to awaken your third eye, you will realize that you have been going through life half-blind. You will see and experience life through a radically different perspective.

This is by no means a new discovery, although it is relatively new to western culture, which continues to regard spiritual practices with much skepticism. But centuries ago, the concept of third eye awakening was already being practiced by numerous civilizations throughout the world. Harnessing the powers of the third eye chakra was the goal of many spiritual practices in ancient Egyptian, Mayan, and Indian traditions, as well as Buddhism, Hinduism, and Taoism.

Sadly, this concept, along with spirituality in general, has never gained raving popularity in the West. We tend to be skeptical of the mystical and the intangible, conditioned as we are to accept only what science tells us about the physical world. The unseen is relegated as being "unreal." And yet, gravity is an unseen force that literally holds the universe together and keeps the earth from hurtling through space. Science has proven this without a doubt. Electricity is an unseen force that has revolutionized the modern world.

Likewise, the chakras are unseen energy centers in our body that regulate many of our physical and mental functions. If their power is harnessed, it can harmonize and balance our bodies and minds.

Why Should We Awaken Our Third Eye Chakra?

Awakening the third eye chakra or attaining enlightenment has long been the pursuit of many spiritual schools. We might argue that it is more relevant today than ever before. Take a moment to reflect on your life: are you truly happy and fulfilled? Are you at peace with yourself? Do you feel that you are living according to your best and highest purpose?

Nine times out of ten, the answer is no. It is ironic that we have countless conveniences and luxuries at our fingertips, and yet, our lives seem to be more hectic and complicated. All the amazing technologies and gadgets designed to make our lives easier are great—so, why are so many of us over-stressed and burned out? We are under constant pressure to compete, to be "super" parents, great partners and spouses, successful career people, and high achievers. We think that when we have achieved those goals, we will be happy.

Ironically, our modern lifestyle creates more worry and anxiety for us. We worry about the future, we fret about our finances, and we fear to lose our jobs or possessions—and the list goes on. Stress has become the norm in our crazy, consumer-driven materialistic culture.

This is where awakening the third eye chakra can change your life: it will enable you to create a calm haven within yourself where the madness of the world outside can never reach you. You will gain the wisdom to understand that the mindless rat race is not your true calling. You will gain more clarity, knowledge, and focus on what is truly meaningful, and start to behave accordingly. In short, you will become your best possible self!

What exactly is the third eye? It has been described as a gateway to non-physical realms of inner consciousness, inner wisdom, and spiritual gifts. It was referred to in the ancient Indian tradition as "the eye of knowledge." This is not knowledge gained from experience and learning in the physical world. It can better be described as an awakening of one's insight and intuition that brings divine wisdom and unleashes amazing psychic abilities.

Awakening the third eye chakra is not some bogus mystical theory. It is not an abstract philosophy. There are very real and concrete steps that you can take to nurture and revive this center of energy that has lain dormant within you for years. In fact, many of us experience short bursts of third eye awakenings without realizing what they are. It is that gut feeling you get about someone or something that turns out to be 100% right. It is that sense of déjà vu where you think, "I've had this exact conversation with this same person before, but we've just met. How is that possible?" It could be a dream about someone you haven't spoken to in years, and a few days later, that person calls you.

We have all had those experiences where the third eye flicks open for a moment, then closes again. These experiences are a sample of what you can expect to experience when you fully awaken and align your third eye chakra.

What This Book Offers

This book will show you how to start your journey to inner peace and higher consciousness by opening your third eye chakra. Whether you are a complete beginner choosing to awaken your inner eye; or you have some experience in spirituality but want to learn more; or you are just simply curious, this book will deliver some great takeaways.

What this book *will not do* is delve into confusing spiritual theories or waste your time with empty platitudes. This is a comprehensive guide packed with practical techniques, exercises, and tips for awakening your third eye chakra. It will prepare you for what to expect, how to understand messages from your third eye, and how to cultivate the gifts of aura reading, psychic visions, and clairvoyance. This book also offers practical advice on how to make these practices part of your everyday life, as well as some precautions you need to be aware of or may need advice on.

The goal is to help you discover your extraordinary gifts, including how to:

- Access and awaken your third eye chakra.
- Nurture and balance your third eye once it is opened.
- Enhance your intuition and insight.
- Harness psychic abilities you never imagined you had, including clairvoyance and aura reading.
- Live with mindfulness.
- Achieve emotional balance and conquer negative emotions.
- Develop deeper relationships with others—and with yourself!
- Become more open-minded and tolerant.
- Reduce stress and anxiety.

- Get rid of negative energy and boost your energy levels.
- Enhance your focus and develop purpose.

What Will You Gain?

Awakening the third eye chakra allows you to access levels of thought and consciousness outside of the five senses. You will develop your "sixth sense," in a way that allows you to experience other realms of your consciousness that have been ignored. The wealth of wisdom existing within this realm will not only enrich your life but transform it.

Does this sound too wild? Well, quantum physics tells us that other realms or "dimensions" do exist. This is what the ancient traditions discovered, now confirmed by modern science, and, hopefully, what you will experience yourself!

What else do you stand to gain by developing this sixth sense? To list all of the benefits requires a whole book in itself. Suffice it to say that your life—and your outlook on life—will be changed forever. You will get a glimpse of just how this will occur as you continue to read this book.

Finally, this is a book about "actionable" spirituality and applicable techniques (with the science and research to back them up). Basically, awakening the third eye chakra is a skill that can be learned, developed, and mastered. The difference is that the way to master this skill is primarily through spiritual methods. Meditation, visualization, and mindfulness techniques will play a big part in your training.

If you are thinking that developing all of these wonderful qualities requires superhuman effort or special abilities, prepare to be surprised. Anyone can learn to awaken their third eye chakra, even children if they are trained to do so early on in life. In fact, if you have children, you may want to consider doing just that. Many of the techniques discussed here can be simplified to suit a child. Awakening the third eye chakra requires nothing more than commitment and practice on your part. This book will guide you through the rest. Now, let's start the journey!

Chapter One: Understanding the Third Eye Chakra

It makes sense that before jumping into the practical work, you should arm yourself with some basic knowledge about the third eye chakra and what awakening it entails. This chapter will provide you with an overview of the third eye chakra and the basics that you need to know before starting out on this life-changing journey.

What Are Chakras?

Chakra is the Sanskrit word for "wheel," sometimes also translated as "wheel of light." This is why in most diagrams and drawings, you will see the chakras depicted as colored circles or spinning discs. In ancient traditions, these non-physical vortexes of energy were thought to be the source of life energy.

Chakras are essentially the energy centers of our body. Their function is to distribute prana (life energy or cosmic energy) in a consistent flow to balance and harmonize the mind, body, and spirit for optimal health and wellbeing. The chakra system distributes this cosmic energy to various areas in our body through pathways called meridians.

Origins of the Chakra System

The earliest recorded mention of the chakra system can be found in the Vedas, a collection of ancient Indian texts, written somewhere around 1500-500 B.C. The chakra system is closely interconnected with the practice of yoga.

The first practical description on how to activate and balance the chakras was written in the 16th century by Swami Purananda. The sixth chapter of his book *Shri-Tattva-Chintamani* describes the chakra system, the functions and associations of each chakra and how to balance and align them. This work was translated and published in 1919 under the title *The Serpent Power* by Arthur Avalon. This is a fairly simple and informative read for anyone seeking more in-depth knowledge about the chakra system.

The Seven Chakras

There are seven main chakras that run through the body along the spine, each with a different color and function. Each chakra vibrates to a specific energy level and this is why they are associated with certain colors or musical notes that resonate best with each chakra to increase its energy. Each chakra is also associated with a specific gland. The following chart provides a basic breakdown:

CHAKRA	LOCATION	COLOR	RELATED GLAND	FUNCTION
Root Chakra	The base of the spine	Red	Gonads	Sense of smell, vitality, money and food
Sacral Chakra	Below naval	Orange	Lymphatic system	Reproduction, sexuality, desire, joy
Solar Plexus Chakra	Upper abdomen	Yellow	Adrenal glands	Professional success and personal advancement

Heart Chakra	Center of the chest	Green	Thymus	Relationships
Throat Chakra	Throat	Blue	Thyroid	Communication, empathy
Third Eye Chakra	Forehead between the eyebrows	Indigo	Pineal	Intuition, higher consciousness
Crown Chakra	Top of the head	Violet	Pituitary	Heightened awareness, transcendence

The seven chakras are responsible for regulating the circuits of energy that flow through—and surround—the body. The gland associated with each chakra is in turn related to a specific organ or organs. When we experience health problems or emotional issues, the most likely cause is that the chakra related to that organ is blocked or unbalanced. Unblocking the related chakra will create a sustained and harmonious flow to the affected organs and promote healing.

CHAKRA	RELATED ORGANS
Root Chakra	Kidneys, spine, testes
Sacral Chakra	Bladder, prostate, ovaries, spleen, gall bladder, kidneys
Solar Plexus Chakra	Upper spine, stomach, bladder, intestines, pancreas, liver
Heart Chakra	Lungs, heart
Throat Chakra	Vocal cords, bronchia, respiratory tract, esophagus, mouth and tongue

| Third Eye Chakra | Eyes, brain, pituitary and pineal glands |
| Crown Chakra | Brain stem and full spinal cord |

We will discuss the functions of each chakra in more detail as well as how to balance the whole chakra system in a later chapter.

An Overview of the Third Eye Chakra

The third eye chakra is located in the center of the forehead between the eyebrows. You have probably seen drawings or statues of ancient Indian deities like Shiva and Buddha with the third eye depicted in this area.

The exact meaning and function of the third eye differs slightly within the ancient traditions, but all of the major philosophies recognized its significance as a supreme source of knowledge and enlightenment.

The Third Eye in Buddhism

Buddhists define the third eye as "the eye of consciousness." Followers are encouraged to work on awakening the third eye in order to see the world through the mind's deeper consciousness, rather than through physical vision and experience.

The Third Eye in Taoism

Several schools of Chinese philosophy, as well as the Japanese Zen School, believe that the awakening of the third eye allows one to become attuned to the vibration of the cosmos. This enables one to gain higher wisdom, deep inner knowledge, and the ability to live in harmony with all things.

The Third Eye in Hinduism

Shiva, the most important of the Hindi gods, is always depicted with the third eye in the middle of his forehead. It symbolizes his great wisdom and ability to see beyond the physical realm. Here is a fun fact: Shiva is also called "Shiva the Destroyer." It is believed that his third eye is so powerful that when he opens it, all duality and illusion in the universe is destroyed.

The Third Eye in Ancient Egypt

The third eye was known to the ancient Egyptians and known for its mystical properties. It is depicted in ancient Egyptian texts as "the eye of Horus." These third eye depictions from ancient Egypt more closely resembled the pineal gland. Interestingly, the pineal gland is closely related to the third eye chakra and is believed by some to be the third eye itself. Interestingly, scientific research may be able to confirm this in the near future.

Basic Facts about the Third Eye Chakra

- It is associated with the color indigo, traditionally thought to be the color of wisdom. Indigo is also associated with the night, when many of our senses become heightened and sharper. This is why the third eye chakra is related to sensory perception as well. When you open your third eye, you will experience sharper hearing, eyesight, and sense of smell. You will learn how to use the indigo color and its derivatives in various ways to raise the vibration of your third eye chakra. You will begin to experience moments of deep insight and clarity.

- On the musical scale, the third eye chakra is believed to resonate with the note A.

- It is associated with the metal silver and the planet Jupiter.

- It is associated with the opening of the mind to higher consciousness, spiritual development, deep intuition, and psychic abilities.

- On the physical level, it is associated with the circadian rhythm, which regulates the sleep-wake cycle.

- It is linked to the pineal gland, and any imbalance of this gland will directly affect the health of the third eye. (We will discuss the importance of this mysterious gland in the next chapter).

• The third eye chakra also determines how you "see" or perceive the world and the people in your life, and how you react to change.

Why Balance the Third Eye Chakra?

Balancing the third eye chakra simply means opening up the obstructions or "blockages" to allow the circulation of energy from the chakra throughout your body.

When the third eye chakra is optimally balanced, you will experience a sense of calm and peacefulness. You will gain a sense of abundance and gratitude for all that you have. You will feel lighter, both physically and mentally, and more in harmony with the world. On a deeper level, as your third eye expands, you will also begin to experience glimpses of what lies beyond the physical realm.

The main causes of blockages in the third eye chakra are our illusions and misperceptions about ourselves and the world around us. These block the intuition and inner guidance that allows us to see through these illusions and misconceptions.

Symptoms of a Blocked Third Eye Chakra

There are certain signs and symptoms that can help you recognize when your third eye chakra is blocked or unbalanced—which it most likely is. If you recognize three or more of these signs in yourself, then it's time to start working on your third eye chakra:

• Lack of motivation.

• Difficulty feeling inspired or creative.

• Feeling cynical and skeptical and unable to see the purpose or meaning of life.

• Poor vision or memory.

• Obstinacy and rigidity in thinking, sometimes even intolerance.

• Fear and mistrust of your intuition.

• Lack of insight.

- Difficulty making decisions.
- Difficulty setting goals.
- Fear of expressing emotions.
- Tendency to overthink.
- Fear of the future and inability to see the future or plan for it.

It is easy to see how all of these symptoms are indeed related to illusions, misconceptions, and irrational fears. Awakening the third eye chakra will give you the clarity and purpose to overcome your illusions.

What to Expect When Your Third Eye Chakra is Opened

Awakening the third eye chakra can lead to many changes, which can differ from person to person, depending on the severity of the blockage. There is no specific benchmark to measure your progress against—you know yourself best, and therefore, you will be able to feel and see these changes when they occur.

Having said that, the most common changes are inner peace and tranquility, greater empathy for others, a sense of purpose, and harmony with the universe. The more dramatic changes include psychic abilities or spiritual gifts.

Precautions to Bear in Mind

Although this is rare, it is possible that the third eye chakra can become overstimulated. If this happens, it can easily be brought back into balance. It is useful to be able to recognize some of the signs and symptoms related to an overstimulated third eye chakra: your perception may become overly heightened so that you perceive things in an inflated or exaggerated manner.

The calming colors of lavender, purple, and lilac are great for balancing an overactive third eye chakra. This can be done through the use of crystals, a chakra pendulum, or wearing jewelry with stones in these colors. Even a relaxing bath with a few drops of lavender essential oil can help restore the balance. Meditating on the color purple is another great technique.

When your third eye begins to open, it is likely that you will have some psychic experiences. It is important that you do not become obsessed with these experiences or expect them to happen all the time. Psychic experiences are not the norm—nor should they be your ultimate goal.

Learn to accept psychic experiences and embrace them when they occur, but don't obsess about it when they don't.

Conclusion

Hopefully, this chapter has given you a basic background about the chakra system and the functions of the third eye chakra.

It is not difficult to understand why it is important to awaken and balance this chakra to improve the balance and harmony in your life; to be in tune with your inner self; and to improve your overall wellbeing.

In Sanskrit, the third eye chakra is also called "Ajna," meaning "perceive" or "beyond wisdom." Releasing the energy of this chakra not only helps us perceive our lives more clearly and without illusion, but to access realms beyond this world that will indeed take us beyond wisdom itself.

Chapter Two: The Pineal Gland: The Science Behind the Third Eye Chakra

Since prehistoric times, almost every religious tradition has been aware of the third eye. It is often depicted in imagery and writing, sometimes in the shape of a pine cone, to symbolize the pineal gland.

No discussion of the third eye chakra can be truly meaningful without illustrating its relationship to the pineal gland. The pineal gland is the gland directly associated with the third eye chakra, but unlike the other chakras, the interdependence here is more pronounced—and actually, somewhat eerie.

To fully understand how to awaken and nurture the third eye chakra, we must understand this vital and mysterious connection. The optimal health of the third eye chakra is directly related to the optimal functioning of its corresponding gland and vice-versa.

It is important to note that while the chakras are invisible centers of energy, their corresponding organs and glands are physical and tangible. Therefore, problems with a particular gland can cause blockages in the corresponding chakra. This is especially true of the third eye chakra and pineal gland relationship.

What is the Pineal Gland?

The pineal gland has remained an enigma and been the subject of controversy for ages. In ancient times, it was regarded as "a mystery gland," and theories abounded about its mystical powers. For this reason, it was sometimes called "the pineal eye."

The pineal gland is a small reddish-gray gland shaped like a pine cone, from which its name is derived. It was first depicted as the symbol of a pine cone by the Sumerians. This pine cone symbol can be seen in the art of many ancient cultures, suggesting that it held great importance.

The pineal gland is about one-third of an inch long and belongs to the endocrine system (the system of hormone-producing glands necessary for various bodily functions). It is located in the midbrain; it is embedded within the crevice between the left and right hemispheres.

For a long time, the pineal gland was regarded as an unimportant vestigial organ that was unworthy of in-depth investigation. Even today, science has not fully discovered all of its functions—but what is known so far signifies its vital importance in the regulation of several bodily functions.

The Function of the Pineal Gland

- Its main function is the production of the hormone melatonin. Melatonin regulates the body's circadian rhythm (sleep-wake cycle).

- Melatonin promotes sexual development in both sexes.

- It induces sleep.

- It connects the nervous system with the endocrine system by converting neural signals into hormone secretion.

- It helps regulate immune system functions.

- Melatonin regulates the mood and helps us adapt to change. It plays an important role in our happiness and contentment.

- It interacts with many other organs, as well as the blood.

- Studies indicate that the melatonin secreted by the pineal gland may affect cardiovascular health and blood pressure, but more research is needed.

- Other studies indicate that the pineal gland may play a role in regulating female hormones and could be linked to irregular menstrual cycles and fertility. Again, more research is needed to confirm this.

The Pineal Gland and the Third Eye

The pineal gland was sometimes actually considered the third eye itself, perhaps because of its location deep in the center of the brain.

French Philosopher René Descartes was so fascinated with the enigmatic pineal gland that he wrote extensively on it, calling it "the seat of the soul" and the area where all thoughts are shaped. The gland was also known to the ancient Greeks, who shared Descartes' view that is was the center of thought.

Although these opinions have been thoroughly dismissed by science, amazingly, recent research may confirm that Descartes and the Greeks were right! A revolutionary study has reported a connection between the pineal gland and a compound called dimethyltryptamine (DMT). This substance is found naturally in many types of plants and has psychedelic properties. It is known to cause psychic visions and profoundly heightened and vivid perceptions.

Clinical psychiatrist Dr Rick Strassman has done extensive research on DMT, after being commissioned by the U.S. government to do research on psychedelic drugs.

During his extensive studies on natural psychedelic substances, including DMT, Dr Strassman made the astonishing discovery that the pineal gland also secretes the substance in certain situations.

In his book *DMT: The Spirit Molecule,* he details all of his truly groundbreaking findings. His theory is that DMT secreted by the pineal gland allows for the life force to transition into this life from another realm (during birth). It also enables the transition of life force from this life into the next dimension (at death). Strassman asserts that DMT is released in the pineal gland during extremely stressful and traumatic situations, such as birth and death.

Strassman describes the pineal gland as "the intermediary between the physical and the spiritual." In other words, the pineal gland has a purpose very similar to the third eye chakra.

Needless to say, Dr Strassman's study has caused immense excitement and debate. Many studies are now underway to uncover the full story of the tiny, enigmatic pineal gland.

The long-ignored pineal gland, like the third eye chakra, may well be the doorway to psychic experiences and other realms. Descartes and the Greeks were not so far off base after all. The pineal gland and its associated third eye chakra may indeed be the seat of the soul!

In the meantime, there is still very little known about the pineal gland and its full spectrum of functions, other than its secretion of melatonin. Let's wait and see what more research tells us in the future.

Ten Fascinating Facts about the Pineal Gland

The pineal gland is thought to be the third eye by many spiritual schools. Here are some facts that may confirm this:

1. The pineal gland stops growing somewhere between one and two years of age. From puberty onwards, it begins to increase slightly in weight.

2. It contains pigment similar to that found in the eyes.

3. It gets its name from the Latin "pinea" which translates as "pine cone."

4. When it is cut open, it appears very similar to an eye.

5. It contains light receptors that are thought to be responsible for inner sight or insight.

6. Unlike other parts of the brain, it is not isolated by the blood-brain barrier and receives a direct and abundant blood flow. The only other body organ which has the same function is the kidney.

7. It appears to be related to near-death experiences, visions, and when overstimulated, to hallucinations.

8. Many scientists consider it to be some form of an eye.

9. In 1886, anatomists discovered that the pineal gland actually contains retina cells, pigment cells and a direct response to light, just like a physical eye.

10. Ancient texts and drawings from almost all cultures of the world regarded it as a third eye.

Calcification of the Pineal Gland

Calcium, fluoride, and phosphorus can build up in the pineal gland over time. These deposits cause what is known as "calcification." A calcified pineal gland can be easily diagnosed with normal x-rays.

Calcification of the pineal gland is more likely to occur when the third eye is dormant—meaning that the majority of people today have some degree of calcification in the pineal gland. An awakened and active third eye chakra keeps the pineal gland healthy, and is the best way to prevent calcification from occurring.

Calcification is basically where a hard, solid ridge builds up around the pineal gland, effectively blocking the door to other realms. It can also cause other physical problems, if ignored. Studies have shown that a calcified pineal gland can cause the following symptoms and disorders:

- Slow production of melatonin, which can wreak havoc on the body's sleep cycle and circadian rhythm.

- A slow or lethargic thyroid, which has its own set of physical problems.

- Low melatonin production may lead to mood swings and even mental disorders.

- Poor blood circulation.
- Weight gain and sometimes obesity.
- Kidney disorders.
- Digestive disorders.
- Confusion.
- Depression.
- Fatigue.
- Poor sense of direction.
- Spiritual disconnection.

How to Decalcify the Pineal Gland

It is possible to "heal" a calcified pineal gland and dissolve the buildup of calcium, fluoride, and phosphate that has accumulated over the years. The methods listed below will also help maintain and promote the health of the pineal gland and prevent calcification from reoccurring.

You may or may not choose to have x-rays to determine whether you have a calcified pineal gland; however, the methods listed below can be followed with or without an official diagnosis. Even if you don't have calcification, these are excellent preventive measures as well has great pineal health boosters.

Avoid excessive intake of calcium. Calcium is important for our health and for maintaining strong bones and teeth. However, some people tend to go overboard and needlessly consume too much.

It is sufficient to stick to the recommended daily intake, which is enough to keep your body in good shape. Avoid calcium supplements as well, as some studies have shown that they can actually do more harm than good. Stick to natural sources of calcium like dairy products, seafood, legumes, and nuts.

Avoid excessive fluoride. Most of our fluoride intake comes from the water flowing through our taps, and the water supplies of most modern cities contain shocking amounts of the chemical. Invest in a special filter to remove fluoride from your drinking water. It is money well-spent. You can also drink alkaline or distilled water.

Another source of fluoride is, of course, toothpaste. Read the labels on toothpaste and opt for a brand with low fluoride—or go natural and alternate between brushing with toothpaste and baking soda every other day.

Get rid of mercury tooth fillings. Mercury is an extremely toxic heavy metal, which, unfortunately, has been used as a base for tooth fillings. This heavy metal resting in an area so close to the brain can cause havoc with the pineal gland.

The good news is that today, many dentists are using fillings that do not contain mercury, so confirm this with your dentists if you are getting a tooth filled. You should also consider removing your old fillings and replacing them with the new non-mercury based ones.

Food. Food choices are one of the best and easiest ways to set the decalcification process into motion. There are a wide variety of foods that work to decalcify the pineal gland and boost its overall health.

Apple cider vinegar, iodine, chlorella, and spirulina are great for decalcifying and preventing calcification. Avocadoes, bananas, watercress, pineapple, and cucumber are your best food choices for a healthy pineal gland.

Reducing your meat intake will also keep a decalcified pineal gland healthy. Meats like pork and beef are highly acidic and not conducive to brain health in general.

Consider using bentonite clay. This is a type of clay that is formed from volcanic ash and has been used throughout history for its detoxifying properties. Bentonite clay has magnetic properties that attract and bind with toxins, especially heavy metals and remove them from the body.

It was used in ancient times to cure various skin conditions and digestive problems. Bentonite clay can be safely ingested, and once inside the body, it attracts and binds with harmful toxins and chemicals, which are then eliminated through the digestive tract.

The clay is sold online and can be found in most health food stores as well.

Love the Sun. The orange rays of the sun (during sunset or sunrise) are extremely beneficial for decalcifying the pineal gland. Taking a walk or going outdoors at these times is a great way to expose yourself to these healing rays.

Eat organic. The heavy metals in pesticides can also be detrimental to the health of the pineal gland and in addition, are very hard to flush out of the body. Eat as organically as possible, or at least make sure your fruits and vegetables are organically grown. Grass-fed beef and organic poultry are highly recommended, as well.

Harness the healing power of herbs. Certain herbs such as mugwort, oregano, alfalfa, dill, and parsley have potent healing properties. Use them often in salads or dips or drink them as herbal teas.

De-stress. This one is just good common sense. Allowing stress to accumulate can lead to very serious physical and mental disorders. Take the time to de-stress regularly by engaging in relaxing activities, exercising, and meditating.

Avoid fluorescent lighting. The pineal gland is very sensitive to light and functions best in natural lighting. Fluorescent bulbs are not part of the natural light spectrum and are, therefore, very disturbing to the pineal gland.

Awaken your third eye chakra. As mentioned before, a dormant third eye chakra is another major cause of pineal gland calcification.

An active third eye chakra will energize and strengthen the pineal gland, keeping these two pathways working together in harmony.

Conspiracy Theory

This is really unrelated to the topic, but it is a fun fact to know. There is actually a conspiracy theory surrounding the pineal gland.

Proponents of this theory are called "anti-fluoride activists." The theory itself has several variations, but in a nutshell, anti-fluoride campaigners believe that fluoride is a brain-altering chemical that is harmful in excessive amounts. Depending on the theory, fluoride either damages the brain cells or the pineal gland over time.

Anti-fluoride activists believe that there has been a conspiracy since World War II to fluoridate drinking water to keep the masses placid and obedient. Who exactly is behind this plan? Again, this varies from "world governments," "Masonic entities" to "the ruling elite." This is commonly referred to as the "mass medication theory."

Another version of the theory claims that chemical companies—in collusion with governments—dump fluoride into our water system as an easy way to get rid of this byproduct (and make money out of it at the same time). This is the "industrial poison" theory.

A possible explanation for these beliefs is that these activists are influenced by the age-old enigma of the pineal gland. The fact that science has yet to uncover all its secrets could lead some people to suspect some sort of diabolical scheme; needless to say, there is no conclusive evidence for such theories, and perhaps it is best to take them with a grain of salt.

Conclusion

Let's conclude this chapter with a remarkable tidbit that illustrates the power of the pineal gland. Science tells us that most animals have a pineal gland, but unlike humans, they make the most of it. While many people have let this important gland become dormant and powerless, certain animals have learned to harness their capabilities in ways the human race has never considered.

We have all seen flocks of birds flying in perfectly-synced unison and wondered how they do it. You never see one member of the flock speeding up and crashing into the bird ahead of it. You never see one bird slowing down and the one behind colliding with it. Every bird in that flock keeps to some invisible formation in a beautiful aerial display.

This is because birds have harnessed the capacity to work *as one mind* through their pineal glands. They actually communicate telepathically. Migrating geese are an excellent example of this.

Animals apparently have the ability to communicate telepathically through the pineal gland, which illustrates the potential of this tiny organ and what it can mean for the human race. Imagine if all humans were able to recognize this power and use it for the common good!

Hopefully, you now have an understanding of how the functions of the pineal gland and the third eye chakra are intertwined. If the third eye chakra has the ability to transcend the physical realm, the spiritual characteristics of the pineal gland enforce and enhance this ability.

So, the first practical step in this guide is to start reviving and detoxifying your pineal gland with the steps listed above. Make sure to eat the "superfoods" suggested; check out the bentonite clay; and filter your water. You will start to feel the difference. You will notice that you have more energy, more clarity and focus, and your sleep will improve. You will feel more uplifted and optimistic and less liable to mood swings and depression. These are all signs of a healthier pineal gland.

In the following chapters, we will start to work on opening the third eye chakra and strengthening its vital relationship with the pineal gland. The two working together in harmony is the first step toward the development of your psychic gifts.

Chapter Three: Laying the Groundwork: Exercises for Opening the Third Eye

Are you ready to open the door to inner awareness and extrasensory experience? This chapter contains fifteen exercises to awaken your third eye, listed in random order. You can start with one or two that resonate most with you, then interchange them or add more to your routine. As you will soon discover, awakening your third eye is not an out of reach fantasy.

Preparatory Steps

As you are preparing to do these exercises, you should be aware of three basic mindsets or qualities that are essential for the exercises to be optimally effective. It is a good idea to practice these mindsets for at least one week to allow them to kick in before you start practicing the exercises.

1. Embrace your intuition.

Prepare your intuition for the amazing insights and information you will begin to receive, by not ignoring or shrugging off thoughts that seem "trivial" or "silly." You must learn to trust your intuition and to listen and accept what your third eye tells you once it starts to expand.

This is even more important if you are someone who has generally been mistrustful of your feelings or if you perceive them as irrational. Try the following to become more in tune with your inner voice:

- Practice lucid dreaming.
- Play guessing games.
- Read tarot cards.
- Practice interpreting your dreams.
- Stop and explore how you are feeling in certain situations or toward people you have just met.

Just keep an open mind, don't dismiss gut feelings, and stop and reflect on the random thoughts that come to you out of the blue; this is usually how you will receive messages from your third eye.

2. Learn to savor the silence.

The exercises and meditations in this book should be practiced in silence. Not necessarily in silent surroundings, although that would be ideal. (You will learn how to deal with noise and distractions in a later chapter). It is about learning to foster and bask in the silence of a tranquil, calm mind.

This is because your third eye will begin to give you access to deeper and subtler messages as your perception becomes heightened. A silent, still mind is necessary for you to be able to hear and sense these messages. They will be almost like a whisper at first until your third eye becomes fully awakened.

Cultivate inner silence with the following:

• Spend quiet time in nature. This could be sitting calmly in a grassy meadow or on a beach, or taking a walk in a quiet park.

• Take a few moments each day to lay down, close your eyes, and just focus on the silence of your mind. Dismiss distracting thoughts by taking a deep breath and continuing just to sit calmly.

• Listen to peaceful music.

• Practice a calming hobby like painting or crafts, where your mind can become totally immersed in what you are doing.

3. Foster your creative force.

A dormant third eye chakra stifles creativity and spontaneity. Fostering your creativity will facilitate the process of opening the third eye. Boost your creative force by engaging in anything creative. Here are some suggestions:

• Dance or sing.

• Finger paint.

• Play with clay.

• Build things with Legos.

• Write poetry.

• Design a handmade card for a friend or loved one.

• Play with children and pick up on their delightful spontaneity!

Creativity helps you let go of rigid logic, overly-rational thoughts, and conventional beliefs of right or wrong. These will really hinder the process of third eye awakening. Your mind needs to be open and ready to accept very unconventional experiences, indeed! The more open you are to the possibilities, the more you will empower your third eye chakra.

Seven Day Plan for Mental Detoxification

It is always best to start with a "clean slate," so to speak. Here is a suggested seven-day plan to clear, de-stress, and detoxify your mind, to make it more receptive to third eye exercises and techniques. Dedicate each day to only practicing the suggested activity, and by the end of the week, you will find that your mind is much calmer and more focused.

Day 1: Get Organized

- Take a few minutes the night before to organize your thoughts and plan your day. Use a computer desktop planner or notebook to write down all of the things you need to do the next day, the times you need to do them, and set an approximate deadline for each task.

- Schedule time for breaks and meals, as well.

- Be prepared for unexpected interruptions, and don't panic if your schedule gets thrown off a little bit.

- This exercise is to help you see that a planned and more structured day can eliminate mental clutter and help you be more focused and productive.

Day 2: Practice Gratitude

Your goal for day two is to count your blessings from the moment you wake up until you lay your head on your pillow at night. Start your day by being grateful that you are here to enjoy it. Appreciate the smell and warmth of your morning coffee and give blessings for your breakfast.

As you go through your day, find things to be grateful for that you have always taken for granted. For example: your nice office; the friendly waitress at the restaurant where you go for lunch; or the pretty view outside your window. How often have you stopped to consider how much better these things make your life?

More importantly, take the opportunity to appreciate your loved ones and remember the joy they bring into your life.

By the time you go to bed, you will be filled with peace, calm, and thankfulness for being so blessed.

Day 3: Go with the Flow

This is the complete opposite of a scheduled day. On day three, your mantra will be: "It is what it is." Don't plan and don't have any expectations. Just take each thing as it comes and deal with it calmly. Don't fly off the handle when anything unexpected comes up, and confront crises and tough situations without panicking, because "It is what it is," and nothing lasts forever.

This exercise helps you put things in perspective and prevents you from obsessing or stressing when things don't go exactly as planned.

Day 4: Be in the Present

Learning to be mindful is key to awakening the third eye chakra, so this is good practice for the exercises you will do later. Pause several times during the day to notice your surroundings and focus on what you are doing.

Focus on the sounds, smells, and sights around you. Become mindful of where you are and the objects around you, such as a painting on the wall, the items on your desk, and the view outside your window. Bring your mind to what you are doing and become fully immersed in the task.

When you catch yourself thinking about picking up the kids at 4:00 p.m. or the pile of laundry waiting at home, bring your mind back to the present.

Needless to say, this is a day when you should avoid multitasking and focus on one thing at a time.

Day 5: Keep the Past in the Past

One of the most mentally destructive things we do as humans is dwell on painful past events. We dwell on conversations and arguments, replaying them over and over in our minds. We hold grudges and resentment toward others whom we blame for our past misfortunes and pain.

On day five, your goal is to catch yourself dwelling on the past and immediately dismiss those thoughts by focusing on what you are doing, and then think positive thoughts.

When you practice this exercise, you will be surprised to discover how much of your day you actually spend living in the past.

Day 6: Think before You React

On this day, you should pause to reflect before speaking or reacting to everything you encounter. Listen to what others are saying and don't respond with the first thing that comes to your mind. Instead, pause, process the information, and respond calmly and appropriately. The same applies to your actions throughout the day. This is a good way to curb impatience and panic and helps you to see things in perspective.

Day 7: Declutter Your Brain

Day seven is for reflecting on the past six days and decluttering your brain of any negative thoughts.

Think only of the positive and pleasurable things that happened throughout the week, what you have accomplished at work, great conversations you had, enjoyable events, and difficult situations you handled successfully. Dwell on these positive thoughts and mentally sweep all of the negative thoughts out of your mind.

You can revisit this exercise every few months to keep your mind clear and balanced. It will not interfere with the third eye chakra exercises and meditations.

Fifteen Exercises for Awakening the Third Eye Chakra

This is a compilation of the most effective exercises to awaken, nurture, and maintain the health of the third eye chakra. You should try each one at least once to get a feel for it.

Exercise 1: Mindful Breathing

This exercise can be done whenever you have five minutes to sit quietly in a comfortable and relaxed position.

- Make sure you are seated or reclining comfortably.
- Close your eyes and take a few moments to let your body relax.
- Inhale slowly through your nose for a count of five. Focus only on the activity of breathing. Feel the air passing through your nostrils and filling your lungs. Feel your lungs expand with air.
- Hold your breath for two or three seconds.
- Slowly exhale through your mouth for a count of five, again focusing on the feel of your breath as it leaves your body.
- Become aware of the tension leaving your body with each exhalation.
- Repeat ten times.
- Note: Breathe deeply from your belly. Shallow breathing will defeat the purpose as it causes stress. Make sure you pull the air deeply into your stomach and release it slowly from there.

This is one of the best exercises for enforcing the silence of the mind. It also helps to cleanse and energize the third eye, balance the whole chakra system, and helps ground perception and awareness. It is also an instant stress reliever.

Mindful breathing can be practiced in many situations, such as in a comfortable chair at home, in the office during a break, or as you are commuting, or sitting in your car.

Exercise 2: African Tongue-Rolling

This is a traditional practice among various African tribes where communing with the spirit world is a sacred rite. They believe that the third eye chakra must be very powerful in order to engage in these rites, and hence, this exercise is commonly practiced to strengthen it:

- Use your tongue to slowly stroke the roof of your mouth from front to back for two-to-three minutes.

- Move your tongue faster along the roof of your mouth and use your voice to make a fluttering sound. Feel the roof of your mouth begin to vibrate. Intensify the movement to increase the vibration as much as possible. This is supposed to "attract the attention of the third eye."

- Continue doing this for three-to-four minutes.

Exercise 3: Touching the Third Eye

The purpose of this exercise is to enforce the intention of the subconscious.

- Place your finger on the third eye chakra in the middle of your forehead and silently state the intention of awakening it.

- Gently massage your third eye in a circular motion and visualize it beginning to pulse and awaken. Continue this motion for three or four minutes.

- Pause every few seconds to gently tap on the third eye two or three times then continue massaging, visualizing the eye as it slowly begins to awaken under your touch.

Exercise 4: Moon-Gazing

Moonlight energizes the third eye, heightens intuition, and sharpens perception.

Of course, moon-gazing is not an exercise that can be done regularly, as it depends on your specific climate and weather conditions. But if you can, you should take advantage of warm, moonlit nights to spread a blanket in your backyard, rooftop, or balcony, and lie back to contemplate the wondrous beauty of the moon and stars. It is a simple and relaxing way to promote silence of the mind while bathing your third eye in nurturing moon rays.

• Lie or sit down and simply gaze at the moon.

• Imagine the moon's light bathing your body and entering into your third eye.

• Acknowledge any thoughts that come to you and try to listen to your third eye.

Exercise 5: Scrying

Scrying is an ancient practice of psychic awareness or second sight. It allows you to "see" in a similar way to the cliché of a sorceress with a crystal ball. But don't worry. You don't have to go out and buy a crystal ball to do this exercise.

Scrying can be done through a variety of methods such as gazing into a pool of water, a mirror, fire—or a crystal ball if it takes your fancy! Gazing at clouds is another great way to practice scrying.

This exercise is great for removing third eye blockages to release energy and enhance inner vision. It has nothing to do with reading the future. It is simply a process of opening the mind to the messages your third eye sends you.

Suggested Items to Use for Scrying

You are probably familiar with the practice of scrying from images you have seen of a sorceress gazing into a crystal ball. However, there are other methods of scrying that are probably more accessible.

• **Mirrors.** Gazing into a mirror is one of the most common methods of scrying.

• **Water.** A simple bowl of water fulfills the same function as a crystal ball. You can drop pebbles or crystals in the water and gaze at the ripples they make.

- **Oil.** You can use regular cooking oil or scented oil; the fragrance will engage your sense of smell and expand your perception. The oil is poured into the water, and you gaze at the movements and shapes that it makes, and the light reflecting off of it.

- **Wax.** This is where heated wax is dripped into a bowl of water. You can simply light a candle and tilt it so that the wax falls into the bowl and hardens.

- **Fire.** Staring into the flame of a candle or a wood fire is a great way to see amazing images and receive amazing messages. It is actually the oldest method of scrying.

How to Practice Scrying

- Gaze intently at whatever you have chosen for the exercise.

- Gently relax your vision and allow it to become a little unfocused.

- Continue to stare into the mirror, water, or fire, until images begin to form.

- Contemplate the images and try to see if you can interpret any messages coming from your third eye.

You may not necessarily see any clear visions or receive specific messages, especially at the beginning. The goal of scrying is to give you a sense of the psychic energy residing within your third eye, and the more you awaken it, the more vivid the images you receive will become—and the more easily you will be able to interpret them.

Exercise 6: Third Eye Visualization

This exercise works to awaken your inner eye by using it to replace your physical eyes.

- Start with simple objects until your third eye is trained to do this with more complex objects.

- An image of a circle, square, or a circle in a vivid color is a good example to start with. You can also choose any simple physical object such as a pencil, a mug, an ashtray, et cetera.

- Stare at the object intently for a few minutes, registering every detail.

- Close your eyes and visualize the object, recreating every detail and color until you can see it in your mind's eye as if you are viewing it physically.

This exercise requires extreme concentration, but over time, it will become easier. You will learn to use your inner eye to recreate visualizations of posters, book covers, and intricate objects so realistically that you will be amazed.

Exercise 7: Projection

This marvelous exercise allows you to travel through time and space – in your mind!

- Choose a place you know well and enjoy visiting. It could be a park, a shop you love, or your favorite restaurant.

- Close your eyes and visualize every detail, then try and imagine yourself in that place as if you were there physically.

- Relive a past event that happened in that place as if it is happening again at the very moment. Try to recall every detail and even the conversations you had. Let yourself be transported back into the past and play out the scene as if you had gone back in time.

- Now, project yourself into the future by imagining either that same place or another place you know well. Visualize what will happen the next time you visit that place, what you will be wearing, what the weather will be like, or people you will meet. Let your mind take you wherever it will, as you project yourself into that future scene.

This exercise awakens your inner senses and gives your third eye a good workout.

Exercise 8: Balasana Yoga Pose

Yoga, in general, is very effective for opening the third eye, but this position is specifically helpful. It is called the "sleeping child" or "child's pose" position.

- Use a yoga mat or a folded blanket or a carpeted floor.
- Lower yourself gently to the floor and sit on your heels.
- Breathe deeply three times.
- Slowly lower your upper body forward until your forehead is touching the floor.
- Do not stretch your arms out in front of you, but keep them lying next to your body, palms up.
- Bring your awareness to your forehead and keep your focus there. Breathe deeply for a few minutes, focusing only on your forehead.
- Very slowly raise your body up again until you are back in the sitting position on your heels.
- Move your head back and rest it on the back of your neck. Keep your eyes looking upwards for a few moments while breathing deeply.
- Repeat the exercise three times.

Exercise 9: Color Visualization

This is one of the best exercises for energizing and unblocking the third eye chakra.

- Sit in a comfortable position and take three deep breaths, allowing the tension to leave your body.
- Close your eyes and visualize a purple or dark blue wheel of energy spinning in the area of your third eye.
- Focus on the ball of energy as it radiates energy into your third eye.
- Continue the exercise for as long as you wish.

Exercise 10: Practice Seeing your Aura

Some people who open the third eye chakra can actually see auras. This is a good way to start practicing while energizing your third eye chakra at the same time. We will discuss seeing auras in more detail later. This is a great exercise for enhancing peripheral vision, which you need in order to see auras.

• Practice this exercise in a well-lit (but not too bright) room and in front of a neutral-colored wall.

• Sit down in front of the wall on the floor or a chair. Stretch your arms toward the wall until they are about 40 centimeters away from the wall and directly in front of your eyes.

• Bring your index fingers together and focus your vision on the point where they are touching.

• Move your index fingers slightly apart, but keep your vision focused on the point where they were touching.

• Extend your vision along at the same point but further away into the distance.

• Continue to focus on the distance, and in your peripheral vision, you should see a faint blue light around your fingers and hands. This is the light of your aura.

• This may not happen the first few times, but with practice, you will be able to see the light and even practice the exercise in total darkness. The main goal of this exercise is to strengthen peripheral vision and energize third eye perception.

Exercise 11: Crystal Exercise

Certain stones and crystals help energize the third eye chakra. Some of these include lapis lazuli, blue sapphire, blue agate, and blue quartz.

• Pick up the stone or crystal and hold it in your hand for a moment.

• Close your eyes and visualize the energy flowing from the crystal to your third eye chakra.

• Feel it enter your third eye, warming it and causing it to tingle.

• Practice this exercise with a different stone each time, letting your intuition guide you as to which one you choose.

Exercise 12: Mindfulness Grounding Exercise

One of the main causes of a dormant third eye is not living mindfully and not being grounded in the present. Thinking too much about the future, ruminating over the past, and living in fantasy causes our third eye to lose perspective because it is not grounded in reality.

You can apply this exercise to anything you do in daily life, but here, let's focus on the activity of eating a meal.

- Sit down before your plate, but don't start eating right away. Instead, close your eyes and focus on the smell of the food for a few moments.

- Open your eyes and begin eating, focusing your attention only on the food you are eating.

- Chew slowly, savoring it, and contemplating the different tastes and textures.

- Feel the food moving down your throat and settling into your stomach.

- Be mindful only of the meal you are eating at the present moment.

You can practice this exercise when folding laundry, washing dishes, or any other mundane task. Rather than letting your mind wander, focus only on what you are doing and let your mind and senses observe and register every detail.

Over time, you will learn to live more mindfully, keeping your third eye grounded in reality.

Exercise 13: Crystal Meditation

For this exercise, you need a small amethyst crystal that can be placed on the area of your third eye chakra.

- Lie down and place the amethyst on your forehead.

- Visualize the energy from the crystal penetrating your third eye and filling it with energy.

- Silently state the intention that you are awakening your third eye.

- Continue the exercise for as long as you wish.

Exercise 14: Third Eye Mantra

The word "Om" is often chanted like a mantra in spiritual practices because it actually matches the vibration of the third eye. It creates healing energy that balances and nurtures the third eye chakra.

- Lie or sit in a comfortable position and focus on your third eye.

- Chant the word "Om" in a monotone voice over and over.

- Feel the vibrations of the mantra flowing into your third eye and visualize it vibrating along with the mantra.

- Practice the exercise for as long as you wish.

Exercise 15: Third Eye Mudra Exercise

- Sit on the floor with legs crossed and back straight.

- Place your palms together in front of you with both thumbs touching and tilted towards your chest. Both of your middle fingers should be touching as well. The rest of your fingers should be bent.

- Inhale deeply through your nose, and as you exhale, utter the mantra "Ksham" while focusing on your brow chakra.

- Repeat seven times.

What to Expect

As your third eye chakra begins to open with these exercises, you will begin to experience a gradual change. It may be almost imperceptible at first, but you will feel it. Don't expect too much early on, however. Give yourself time, stay open, and be patient. After all, your third eye has been dormant all your life. It needs time to open up and slowly come to life. You can expect to experience some of the following:

- A slight headache when you wake up in the morning.

- Pressure in the area of the third eye chakra. The pressure may be quite strong as if something is pressing down on your brow, or it could be slight. This is a sign that your third eye is expanding.

- A tingling sensation in the third eye area.

- You may hear slight popping sounds in your head at intervals during the day.

- You may have increased sensitivity to bright light.

- Heightened senses where you will see, feel, smell, and hear things with a new level of awareness.

- As your third eye becomes activated, it will be more perceptive of toxins in foods. You may naturally find yourself shunning certain foods while choosing ones that nourish and nurture your body and your third eye. In other words, your third eye awakening will make you more health-conscious!

- You will become aware of the improvement in concentration and focus.

When you begin to experience some of these symptoms, you can be certain that your third eye has been opened. Congratulations! Your metamorphosis has begun!

These exercises should be practiced regularly on a daily basis, if possible, as well as alternated. Get creative with combinations, choosing to practice two or three exercises for a week or two before switching to a new set. Explore which ones work best with you.

A word of advice here; don't rush it. Be patient and give the exercises time to work. There is no time frame for expected results. Some people may start to experience symptoms of the third eye awakening after only a week. With others, it may take months. Just continue with the exercises as well as the additional techniques you will learn in the next chapter.

Chapter Four: Meditation: The Cornerstone of Third Eye Awakening

If music is food for the soul, meditation is the most potent food for the third eye chakra. In fact, meditation is the best food for any endeavor in spiritual awakening. In fact, some of the exercises discussed in the previous chapter are actually "mini-meditations." But opening the inner eye chakra requires taking it to a higher level with more intense meditation sessions. Meditation should be practiced alongside the exercises.

What Exactly is Meditation?

Meditation is a skill that can be learned and honed, just like any other skill we try our hand at. It does not require any special talents. On the other hand, it also needs to be approached without skepticism.

If you are new to meditation, you may feel a bit awkward and uncomfortable at first. However, the majority of people who experience the joys of meditation quickly learn to love it as a relaxing and enriching activity.

Meditation is basically an age-old practice established in ancient Indian traditions. It is practiced with the goal of opening the mind for deeper intuition and perception. There are also several very powerful meditations developed specifically to open the third eye and strengthen the pineal gland.

Meditation also helps you control your thoughts and your mind, putting you, as the proponents of Buddhism believe, in control of your life. This is an extremely empowering gift to have. So many things in life are out of our control—but by learning to control our thoughts, we can respond to situations wisely and calmly and make better choices. This skill becomes even more pronounced when your third eye chakra is awakened.

Meditation develops clarity and improves concentration and is possibly one of the best ways to relieve stress. These are just a few of the benefits of meditation. All of the physical and mental benefits—as well as the research that confirms them—are just too numerous to list here.

How does Meditation Work?

When you meditate, your brain enters into an alpha wavelength state, (which is different from the normal beta wavelength state that the brain resonates with). In this quiet and relaxed state, the mind becomes more open to receiving subtle messages and insights from our third eye. The regular practice of meditation allows you to enter more and more easily into the alpha wavelength state and over time, you can receive deeper wisdom, knowledge, and information from the non-physical realm. It also helps strengthen spiritual gifts.

Types of Meditation

The types of meditation are varied and diverse. Zen meditation, Vispana meditation, mindfulness meditation, transcendental meditation, Taoist meditation, and mantra meditation are some of the most popular. There is also a type of meditation for almost anything, from relieving pain and stress to meeting your higher guides. But ideally, meditation should be approached with the goal of achieving inner calm and deeper awareness—and the sheer bliss of just being able to forget the world and relax.

Meditations for the Third Eye

Meditation allows us to switch off the thinking, logical mind. When the mind is quietened and enters an alpha level wavelength state, it then becomes a filter for subtle insights and messages from the third eye.

All types of meditation are effective for opening the third eye. Guided meditation and any sort of mindfulness meditation will work very well. However, the following are the most powerful for opening and nurturing the third eye.

Meditation 1: Trataka Meditation

This is an ancient meditation derived from the Tantra and Hatha yoga practices. In Sanskrit, Trataka means "to gaze" or "to look."

• This meditation requires you to sit perfectly still on the floor with legs crossed in the lotus position. If this is not comfortable, sit in a straight-backed chair where you can keep your spine straight.

• Close your eyes and breathe deeply from your belly for two-to-three minutes until your body is completely relaxed.

• Focus deeply on the area of your third eye chakra. Continue to focus on the area for a few moments.

• With both of your eyes still closed, draw them upwards towards the inner eye chakra as if you are looking at it. You may feel a strain in your eyes as you try and hold them in that position. You will know that it is the correct position when you feel your eyes "lock" slightly above the bridge of your nose, and the position does not feel too strained.

- Keep your closed eyes in that position and slowly start counting backward from 100 (with about two seconds between each count).

- Keep your closed eyes focused on the third eye chakra until you have finished counting backward to zero.

- Draw your eyes back to their normal position and breathe deeply three times to ground yourself. Allow your eyes to return to their normal movement.

- Feel yourself become grounded and open your eyes. The meditation should last between ten-to-fifteen minutes.

Some people report that when doing this meditation, they can actually see their thoughts as if seeing a dream. You may feel warmth in the area of the inner eye, which indicates that it is attracting energy. In addition, not only is this a very powerful meditation for awakening the third eye, but it is also a great workout that keeps the eyes healthy.

Note: This meditation should be practiced in moderation to prevent the over-activation of the third eye chakra. Once a week will be enough to keep everything in balance.

Meditation 2: Body Scan Meditation for Third Eye Intuition

This meditation is specifically oriented toward increasing your intuition through the third eye chakra.

- Sit in a comfortable position with your back straight.

- Close your eyes and do the mindful breathing exercise in order to ground yourself. This should take two-to-three minutes, or until all the tension is released from your body and you feel completely relaxed.

- Start the body scan from the very top of your head or the crown chakra. Focus on this area until you begin to notice the sensations there. This could be tingling, pressure, a slight warmth, burning, or buzzing. Don't worry if you don't feel anything the first couple of times you practice this meditation. Your mind will become trained to pick up on these sensations over time.

- When you are ready, move down to the whole forehead area from the front to the back of your head. Focus on this area—again, noticing any sensations there.

- When you are ready, move down to the eyes, then the nose, the area above the mouth then the mouth itself. Spend a few minutes on each area and notice the sensations.

- Continue the body scan by moving downwards and exploring every part of your body; chin, neck, shoulders, arms, torso, top of the stomach, lower belly, upper thighs, legs, and finally end with the feet.

- Do not react to or judge any negative sensations that you may feel. Simply acknowledge them and move on.

- If you want, you can repeat the body scan starting once again from the top of your head.

The meditation heightens the intuition by making you more aware of the subtle sensations in your body. You may receive certain insights or "aha!" moments as you are meditating—or even days after the meditation.

Meditation 3: Golden Ball of Light

- Sit in the lotus position or a comfortable chair with your back straight.

- Breathe deeply and feel the tension leave your muscles with every breath.

- Visualize a warm stream of energy flowing through your body from the top of your head down to your toes. Continue to visualize and feel this energy slowly circulating around your body.

- Next, direct your focus to the third eye chakra and the warm energy filling the space between your brows.

- Visualize the energy coming together to form a rotating ball of golden light in the center of your third eye chakra.

- Focus on the rotating ball and the beautiful golden light that emanates from it.

- When you feel ready, allow the light to expand until it fills all of your third eye chakra. Visualize it expanding slowly until it finally emerges out of your forehead in a bright ray of incandescent golden light.

- Gaze at the beautiful ray of light with your inner eye and notice any colors or pictures that appear within it.

- Simply acknowledge what you see without judgment.

- Now, still gazing into the light with your third eye, ask your third eye if it has a message for you. Take as much time as you need.

- When you are ready, bring yourself back to reality with deep breathing and slowly open your eyes.

Again, don't worry if you don't see anything the first few times you practice this meditation. The more you advance, the stronger the ray of light will become as well as the images and messages from your third eye.

Meditation 4: Third Eye Awakening and Decalcifying the Pineal Gland

- Sit in a comfortable position and allow your body a few moments to settle and relax.

- Close your eyes, take a deep breath, and hold it for as long as you can, feeling the fullness in your lungs. Exhale slowly through your mouth.

- Bring your full focus to the third eye chakra. If it helps, you can visualize it as a small ball of light.

- Allow your senses to become vividly and intensely aware of everything around you; any sounds in the background like voices or the hum of electrical appliances, the seat beneath you, the feel of your clothes against your skin, and any smells that may come to you.

- Allow your senses to fully experience all of these things while dismissing any thoughts about them.

- Visualize your third eye absorbing and processing all of these sounds, smells, and sensations.

- When you are ready, end the meditation by taking a few deep breaths.

This meditation can be practiced daily. It energizes both the third eye chakra and the pineal gland and heightens awareness and the senses.

Meditation 5: Mindfulness Breathing Cues

This is great meditation to keep you grounded throughout your day and regularly mindful of your third eye.

- Choose a certain cue from your daily life, such as whenever you look in the mirror or brush your teeth; when your phone rings or you have ended the call. It could be every time you look out of the window or hear a dog bark or a car horn. Just choose a cue that occurs regularly in your daily life—ideally, more than one.

- Each time they come up, breathe mindfully for a few minutes while focusing on your third eye chakra.

- Repeat the exercise whenever the cue occurs.

- This exercise allows you to relax and ground your overactive mind while also checking in with your third eye.

Tips to Get the Most out of Meditation

Here are a few suggestions to help you meditate better. These are not mandatory rules but just useful tips to consider.

Place. The ideal place to meditate should be relaxing and welcoming, with as little noise or disturbance as possible. It does not necessarily have to be indoors. Meditating in nature to the sounds of birds singing or waves sweeping onto the shore is a wonderful experience. The choice is up to you: just a calming environment that resonates with you.

Time. It is best if you are able to meditate at the same time each day; having a consistent meditation schedule really helps to ground your mind and creates a regular pattern of time-out for the body and mind. Many people find that having a regular meditation schedule gives them something to look forward to during a hectic day. Their meditation time is a quiet, energizing haven from the havoc of daily life.

Position. Whether you choose to sit on the floor or in a chair, the important thing is that you are totally comfortable. The ideal position is one where you can nod off if you want you. Always give your body time to settle down and relax before you start, as fidgeting during the meditation will break your focus.

- Try to clear your mind. Connecting with the third eye chakra and receiving information from the higher plane requires extreme clarity and calmness of the mind. This is easier said than done, especially if you are new to meditation. The best way to maintain clarity is to remain focused on the third eye for as long as possible during each meditation.

- Coming out of a meditative state is just as important as entering it. Never just open your eyes and jump up. Always bring your focus back to the physical world slowly and ground yourself with a few deep breaths until you are fully aware of your surroundings.

- Take your time. Each meditation should last for at least 30 minutes.

- Wear loose, comfortable clothing, and no shoes.

- Don't be alarmed when you suddenly receive a poignant message or thought, from your third eye. This may disrupt your concentration.

- Learn how to sit in the proper lotus position as it allows the best alignment of the body.

- Turn off cell phones, TVs, and other sources of distraction.
- Feel free to explore other forms of meditation such as guided meditation and meditating to nature sounds or music, or meditation that incorporates physical movement.
- Enjoy the experience.

Conclusion

A calm mind actually vibrates at a frequency that resonates with the frequency of intuition. The more you meditate, the more your mind will learn to become tranquil and quiet, allowing intuition to be heard more clearly. As your third eye begins to open and receive energy, so will your senses. You will begin to develop crystal clear perception, as well as more and more moments of powerful intuition.

You will find yourself living more in the present moment, as these meditations are also great for boosting mindfulness. These gradual changes will be all the motivation you need to make meditation a part of your daily routine.

Chapter Five: The Third Eye Chakra and Everyday Life: How to Nourish Your Third Eye

Awakening the third eye and healing the pineal gland is not the end of the journey. It is an ongoing process of balancing, strengthening, and nurturing the third eye chakra in order to keep it open and energized. Your personal improvement and the attainment of your highest self is a perpetual work in progress. This chapter will discuss a variety of methods for keeping the third eye chakra healthy.

Thankfully, these methods and techniques can be easily incorporated into your lifestyle. The idea is that whichever of these methods you choose to adopt, they should become habits that go hand in hand with meditation. The result will be a powerful and effective routine that allows you to nurture your amazing third eye continually.

Third Eye Chakra: Nourishing Foods

The third eye chakra is related to the spiritual realm rather than the physical realm. This may lead you to think that it is not influenced by your physical activities, namely, the food that you eat. In fact, there are a number of specific "superfoods" that can keep the third eye chakra balanced and unblocked. Eating a combination of these foods keeps your intuition strong, and your perception open.

Additionally, the third eye resonates with beauty. Believe it or not, the way you arrange your food on your plate, and the integration of different colors can actually bring joy to your third eye. Luckily, the list of foods that promote third eye chakra health is long and varied, with something in it for everyone. You do not need to go on a restrictive diet or deprive yourself in any way. Just make sure you eat as much of the following foods as you can:

1. Indigo, violet, and purple-colored foods are good for the pineal gland and in turn, for the third eye chakra. They are also great for regulating blood pressure and are powerful antioxidants that keep your brain performing at optimum health. These include:

- Eggplant.
- Purple grapes.
- Blueberries.
- Figs.
- Purple kale.
- Prunes.
- Plums.
- Purple onions.
- Raisins.
- Purple cabbage.
- Blackberries.

The color pigments in these foods are said to represent dreams, inner thoughts, and inner harmony with the universe.

2. Dark chocolate enhances brain clarity and contains serotonin, a mood-boosting hormone. Try having a piece before you meditate to boost your focus and enhance your enjoyment.

As a matter of fact, go ahead and have as much dark chocolate as you want when you are in the process of awakening your third eye chakra.

Note: The keyword here is "dark" chocolate, not milk or white chocolate.

3. Nuts and seeds are known as being powerful brain nutrients that help with focus and clarity. Pumpkin seeds and almonds are specifically recommended.

4. Fish contains Omega-3 fatty acids, another great brain nutrient that enhances attention and concentration. Try to eat fish at least two times a week when you are working on opening your third eye and once a week after that.

5. Herbs and spices maintain nervous system health and enhance the senses. Poppy seeds, mugwort, juniper, rosemary, and mint are especially potent. Turmeric has been used since ancient times as well to promote overall brain health.

6. Drinking plenty of water is something we all know we should do, but how many of us actually remember to drink enough throughout the day? It is important to keep your body hydrated throughout the day to keep your mind clear and focused. Water is also the best way to help the body regularly flush out toxins. Always drink a glass of water before you meditate.

In general, a sensible, healthy diet containing plenty of fresh fruits, vegetables, and healthy fats will keep the whole chakra system open and balanced—and keep you in better health.

Physical Exercise and Nature

This is a no-brainer. A healthy body equals a healthy mind, which leads to a balanced chakra system. You may already be practicing some form of physical exercise or engaging in a specific sport, which is great.

Any form of exercise will keep the energy flowing and your chakras balanced. However, you may want to consider the following physical activities that are specifically in harmony with third eye health:

Dance. Dance heightens creativity and perception while also toning the body. Any form of dance is beneficial for third eye health, including dance-style aerobics.

Gymnastics. Exercises that challenge your balance and coordination are excellent for balancing the chakras.

Yoga. Yoga is, by far, the best physical exercise for your third eye. This is because yoga movements and positions are specifically geared to open up the chakra system and allow a sustained energy flow between all of the chakras. It also promotes physical flexibility and tones the body. Consider taking a beginner's yoga class if this resonates with you.

Nature. Any kind of exercise you can practice outdoors in nature is wonderful for third eye chakra health. Hiking, swimming, climbing, nature walks, and cycling are the perfect activities to promote physical and spiritual health. You will get the benefit of fresh air, the inner peace of communing with nature, and a good workout for your muscles.

Keep a Dream Journal

Having psychic dreams is one of the most significant signs that your third eye is open. When it awakens, it sends vibrations through your system that enables the physical body to separate from the act of dreaming, allowing the dreams to come straight from the third eye.

While some people can remember their dreams very vividly, others only remember vague details or can't remember their dreams at all.

However, the third eye awakening usually makes the dream experience more vivid, so you can expect to remember your dreams quite clearly.

Keeping a dream journal will allow you to monitor your dreams to recognize any meaningful messages or symbols. Reviewing the content and development of your dreams will also help you to separate normal dreams from psychic ones.

Normal vs. Psychic Dreams

Oftentimes, our dreams have no meaning. Psychic dreams are when we are given clear messages from our third eye about certain people or future events. Look for the following in your dreams:

- Things that hold strong symbolism or meaning for you. This is the third eye's way of alerting you that the dream is different.

- Psychic dreams are surprisingly vivid. You can recall every detail clearly. The next time you have such a vivid dream, it could very well be a message from another realm.

This is why keeping a dream journal can be extremely helpful. It is a great way to review the progression of your dreams as your third eye chakra awakens. You will learn to recognize dream patterns and analyze dreams that do not conform to the pattern, as they may contain messages.

Keeping a dream journal requires a few minutes of your time each morning. As soon as you wake up, record any dreams you remember from the night before. Try to remember as many details as possible.

For each dream, write down any personal symbolism that you feel is important and what you think it means.

On days when you can't remember your dreams, simply record the date without an entry.

Every week or two, review your entries and look for patterns in your dreams, recurring symbols, and possible messages.

Indigo light

Indigo light is the light associated with the third eye chakra. It is also called Royal Blue. Indigo is the color of inner wisdom and deep knowing and opens us up to experience special spiritual gifts.

To nurture the third eye chakra with indigo light, we must turn to the night. A starlit or moonlit night is the best way to expose your whole body to this powerful color. Stargazing, moon-gazing, and meditating under the night sky are ideal ways to bask in the miraculous power of indigo light.

Using Third Eye Colors in Your Home

The color indigo is a combination of the two colors violet and deep blue. Surrounding yourself with these colors in your home (and in your office or other personal space) will ensure that your third eye is constantly exposed to its associated colors and their healing vibrations at all times. This will keep the third eye chakra unblocked and healthy because if you remember, it loves beauty and recognizes its associated colors as beautiful.

Incorporate hues of indigo, purple, and blue into your home décor wherever you can. This could be in wall art, rugs, pillows, curtains, or bedspreads. If you naturally love these colors, you can even use them in furniture or as the colors of walls.

You can also incorporate indigo, dark blue, and purple into your wardrobe and wear jewelry that contains precious or semi-precious stones in these colors. Silver is the metal that resonates best with the third eye, so silver jewelry embedded with these stones is a good choice.

Consider Binaural Beats

Binaural beats are specifically designed soundtracks that help your brain enter into a specific wavelength state. You must listen to them through headphones. The tracks are designed to send a specific tone or sound frequency to the right ear and a different tone to the left ear.

The two tones work together to help your brain settle into the desired wavelength. Your brain actually processes the two frequencies then creates a third frequency, which is the binaural beat.

Binaural beats are used to boost brain focus, increase productivity, and alleviate depression and anxiety, and to promote better sleep quality. Research on this form of "sound therapy," if you will, is rather inconclusive.

However, you may want to give binaural beats a try. Users have reported better quality sleep and relief from stress and anxiety. Binaural beats can help promote third eye chakra energy simply by allowing the brain to vibrate at a calmer frequency. It is highly unlikely that binaural beats will be very beneficial on their own, but taken in combination with meditation and other techniques, they may be perfect for you.

The best way is to experiment with different frequencies and see what happens. There are a variety of tracks available online as well as binaural beat apps, which are pretty inexpensive.

Aromatherapy

Essential oils are wonderful on many levels. Skeptics see them as a kind of glorified perfume, but actually, science has confirmed their therapeutic properties through hundreds of studies. The olfactory nerves are directly connected to the brain and when essential oils are inhaled, they are very quickly transmitted to the area, where their healing properties very quickly take effect.

Essential oils have calming, energizing, and pain-relieving qualities that range from calming anxiety, alleviating depression, and promoting sleep, to increasing focus—among other things.

It goes without saying that certain essential oils are extremely beneficial to the health of the third eye chakra. Their wonderful fragrances will cleanse, nurture, and balance, while filling your home with a subtle fragrance that everybody will love. Try the following essential oils:

- Nutmeg.
- Sandalwood.
- Myrrh.
- Grapefruit.
- Lavender.
- Chamomile.

How to Use Essential Oils

- Essential oils can be used in a diffuser so that you inhale the scent.
- They can be used in a warm bath for a refreshing and relaxing experience.
- Try spraying bed linen with a light mist of essential oil, so that you can inhale the fragrance as you sleep. You can also place a cotton ball soaked in a few drops of oil on your nightstand.
- Use essential oils during meditation for a deeper experience.
- Use a few drops on your inner elbows. Its fragrance will remain with you throughout most of the day.
- Put a drop of essential oil directly on your third eye chakra.
- You can combine two or three of the oils listed above for variety. Play around and see which ones resonate the most with your senses.

Note: always use a carrier oil when using essential oils directly on the skin and be very careful that it doesn't get into your eyes.

Consider Yoga

We touched on yoga lightly in a previous section. Yoga is a vast realm consisting of various schools and practices.

However, if you wish to consider yoga as an additional subject, here are the basics you need to know:

- Yoga has been used since ancient times to heal, open, and balance the chakra system.

- There are specific yoga positions or "asanas" that are used to open and unblock the third eye chakra. Most of these asanas can be practiced by beginners.

There are dozens of simple yoga techniques for beginners on YouTube: so, instead of rushing out to sign up for a class, try practicing along with some of these videos. (Search for yoga postures designed to open the third eye chakra). If you feel that yoga is something you can get into, consider a beginner's class.

Use Crystals and Stones for Third Eye Chakra Healing

Crystals and stones contain vibrational energy that resonates with the various chakras. Use crystals and stones in the colors associated with the third eye chakra to enhance intuition and nurture your mind's eye with cleansing energy.

The following stones and crystals are recommended:

Amethyst. This precious gem has been used traditionally for healing the third eye chakra. It is also believed to enhance wisdom.

Sodalite. This dark blue stone stimulates the pineal gland and helps develop psychic gifts. It also promotes intuition and clarity.

Purple Fluorite. This is a semi-precious stone that promotes clarity of thought and increases intuition.

Indigo Kyanite. This stone contains powerful energy for the pineal gland and helps develop psychic gifts. It also works to balance and align the whole chakra system.

Black Obsidian. This beautiful crystal is used to promote the balance of the third eye chakra.

Lapis Lazuli. This beautiful stone is perfect to wear in jewelry, such as earrings or rings. It contains wonderful healing properties for the third eye chakra and also calms the mind.

Moldavite. This is a semi-precious stone with a dark green color. Although not directly related to the third eye chakra, its vibrational energy helps clear negative thoughts and cleanse all of the chakras.

Azurite. This is another blue stone that helps develop psychic abilities. It also helps promote deep meditative states and is good to hold in your hand or keep it beside you when meditating.

Stones and crystals can be worn in jewelry or carried in your pocket or handbag, held in your hand or placed directly on the third eye chakra during meditation.

You can purchase non-precious purple and indigo-colored crystals and place them in bowls around your home or in your office. Place them on your third eye chakra for a few minutes even when not meditating, to enjoy their healing energy.

Practice Affirmations

Affirmations are statements that you repeat to yourself in order to empower your mind and replace limiting beliefs with positive ones. They target any area of your life that you want to improve, such as self-confidence, food addictions, overthinking, and productivity, among other things. Likewise, positive affirmations can be used to heal, nurture, and empower the third eye chakra and expand your consciousness.

Affirmations basically work to rewire your brain. When repeated over and over again, the brain learns to believe they are true. It creates neural pathways related to these affirmations, which it perceives as truths. The brain then acts upon those truths, changing your perception and behavior. This is a process called neuroplasticity, where your brain literally learns to enforce a certain belief, and trigger your actions and emotions accordingly. Suffice it to say that affirmations are not a bogus fad but very powerful tools that are used in many fields of psychotherapy as well as in various rehabilitation programs.

Affirmations have three basic rules that need to be followed:

- They should be stated out loud. Not necessarily in a loud voice. Whispering them to yourself is fine; as long as they are physically uttered.

- They should be stated with conviction.
- They should always be in the present tense (and sometimes in the future tense) but never in the past tense.

Some proponents stress that affirmations should be stated while standing in front of a mirror and looking at yourself in the eye. However, this is not carved in stone and understandably, may just feel too awkward for some people. If you are new to affirmations, expect to feel some awkwardness at first. Just stick to it, and you will soon learn to repeat them with purpose and complete conviction.

For the third eye chakra, affirmations should focus on spirituality, insight, and intuition. Here are some examples:

"I follow my intuition and know that it will lead me to my higher purpose."

"I am insightful and intuitive."

"I always dwell in the present moment."

"I completely trust and allow my inner eye to give me guidance."

"With each day, my inner eye becomes more empowered."

"I allow my inner gifts to come freely to me."

"I feel more empowered as my third eye blossoms."

"I expand my awareness through my third eye."

"I nurture my spirit."

"I am open to the wisdom of my third eye."

"I trust that my life is unfolding exactly as it should."

"I am in alignment with the divine universal wisdom."

"I honor my intuition."

"I release all illusions."

"I am connected with my higher self."

"Each day, I am enhancing my psychic gifts and abilities."

"I have complete clarity of mind in all that I do."

These examples should give you an idea of how affirmations should be said. Choose three or four and make sure to repeat them whenever you can throughout the day—the more often, the better. Post them on your fridge or on your computer desktop, where you can see them frequently and remember to repeat them. Repeat the affirmations you have chosen for one week, then pick a new list to repeat for another week, and so on. And by all means, feel free to write your own affirmations to work on the areas you feel are important to you.

Conclusion

Experiment with the additional techniques discussed in this chapter—or all of them—to make your transformation more powerful. Some of the techniques like diet and exercise are just good common sense. Others, like yoga and affirmations, require practice and commitment. But all of them are powerful additions to your meditation and exercise routine and are not difficult to adopt as part of your lifestyle. Get creative, have fun experimenting with essential oils and crystals, enjoy a relaxing evening outdoors stargazing, and unleash your creativity by adding third eye chakra colors to your home and wardrobe. And in the process, be amazed at the changes you will begin to experience.

Chapter Six: Balancing the Seven Chakras

The third eye chakra does not work completely in isolation. It is part of the overall chakra system that runs through our bodies. The good health of the whole chakra system is therefore vital if we want to awaken the third eye successfully.

Centuries before science was known, ancient cultures understood that all living things had a life force flowing through them. The source of this cosmic energy or life force was the chakra system. This cosmic energy or life force is called "prana." Ancient cultures believed that the chakras worked together to regulate the flow of prana. The chakras derive this life force from the divine energy of the cosmos, which is continuously recharging them.

The seven chakras are non-physical energy centers that run vertically along the body like a circuit, through which cosmic energy flows.

What is the Purpose of the Seven Chakras?

The seven chakras are aligned from the top of the head to the base of the spine. Their function is to connect the physical body with the spiritual body by regulating the flow of cosmic energy through a network of meridians.

Why Balance the Chakras?

Our body and mind are interdependent. Both are influenced by our own energy. The chakra system is a brilliant compartmentalization of the prana energy fields that can affect us physically and emotionally. This is why the chakras need to be aligned and balanced.

Stress, anxiety, emotional issues, and health problems can cause the chakras to become blocked so that prana can no longer move freely between the chakras. As a result, we may experience many symptoms of this unbalance, such as emotional isolation, depression, stifled creativity, and mental rigidity, in addition to various physical problems.

Keeping the chakras open and balanced allows prana to flow freely through your body, keeping you healthy physically and spiritually. Learning about the chakras will allow you to be attuned to the signs and symptoms that one or more of them is blocked, and what you can do to balance them.

The Seven Chakras

Just like the third eye chakra, the other six are believed to have specific functions and associations depending on their location.

The 1st Chakra: Root Chakra (Muladhara)

In Sanskrit, the word "mula" means "root," while the word "adhara" means "support." It is located at the base of the spine, and its function is to "root" or connect your energy with the earth. In other words, it keeps you grounded, and this is very aptly named.

The root chakra is associated with basic survival. This means food, water, shelter, and clothing at a very basic level, to protect you from the elements. Today, we might add to that financial security, career security, and health. When the root chakra is balanced, it gives you a sense of security and gratitude for all of the material things you have that make you safe and comfortable. When it is blocked or overactive, the result is fear, worry, insecurity, and irrational panic about survival.

The root chakra is associated with the color red.

The 2nd Chakra: Sacral (Svadhisthana)

The Sanskrit translation is "place of the self," and it symbolizes your identity and all of the different ways in which you express that identity. This chakra's function is to enrich your life by activating and enforcing your creativity. It is the source of a creative prana that allows you to have fun and enjoy the pleasures of life.

When this chakra is balanced, you will enjoy all of the good things that life has to offer; friendship, a rich social life, good food, music, and art.

If it is blocked, you may find yourself feeling lifeless and sapped of energy and vitality. If it is overactive, you may overindulge, especially in food, which can lead to bingeing or obesity. The chakra is usually the root of many kinds of addictions as well, when it becomes overactive.

The sacral chakra is located directly under the belly button and extends to the middle of the stomach. It is associated with the color orange.

The 3rd Chakra: Solar Plexus (Manipura)

In Sanskrit, Manipura means "lustrous gem." This is where your inner strength, resilience, and self-confidence reside. The solar plexus chakra fuels you with the confidence and strength to overcome adversity and avoid harmful or unpleasant situations. It is basically the seat of your resilience.

When this chakra is blocked, we tend to become indecisive, overwhelmed, and unable to cope with difficult situations. When it is overactive, there may be a tendency to become overconfident, to make rash decisions, or to rush head-on into things without thinking them through.

It is located in the center of the belly and is associated with the color yellow.

The 4th Chakra: Heart (Anahata)

The Sanskrit translation of anahata is "unhurt." This chakra's function is to foster your feelings of love, compassion, kindness, and empathy. It is also associated with physical and mental health as well as healing.

As the middle chakra, it has a special significance; it connects the lower chakras associated with the physical realm, to the upper chakras associated with the spiritual realm.

When the heart chakra is balanced, all is well with you and the world. You are in perfect harmony with the universe, and you radiate love, tolerance, and kindness to everyone around you.

Symptoms of an unbalanced heart chakra include selfishness and a tendency to over-indulge. It can also create feelings of jealousy and envy. On a physical level, heart palpitations, frequent heartburn, unhealthy attractions, and destructive relationships are symptoms of imbalance.

It is located in the center of the chest, exactly above the physical heart, and its associated color is green.

The 5th Chakra: Throat (Vishuddha)

Vishuddha literally means "very pure" in Sanskrit. It symbolizes the voice of your higher self and your truth. It allows you to be honest fearlessly and always to speak the truth. It also relates to the expression of thought and allows you to speak articulately and knowledgeably.

When the throat chakra is not in balance, we may find ourselves feeling insignificant, unheard, or ignored. Having trouble articulating the proper words in a given situation is another symptom of imbalance. Physical symptoms include throat infections and problems with teeth, gums, and sinuses. Sometimes, this chakra can become overactive, in which case, a person may speak too loudly or have a tendency to interrupt others.

As its name indicates, it is located in the throat area, and its color is blue.

The 6th Chakra: Third Eye (Ajna)

No need for further details here!

The 7th Chakra: Crown (Sahaswara)

The translation from Sanskrit is "thousand-petaled," and it symbolizes pure spiritual and conscious energy. It is believed to be one's source of connection to the cosmos. This sacred chakra is commonly depicted as a lotus flower.

It is not easy to achieve a perfectly balanced crown chakra. In fact, it is impossible to open it completely according to ancient philosophies, because the levels of consciousness it opens up are beyond human capacity.

The crown chakra is associated with extreme higher consciousness, the liberation of limiting beliefs, feelings of bliss and ecstasy, and communion with the divine. The Tantric school of philosophy believes that the crown chakra connects us with the eternal. It is the connecting point between the present, the future, and the infinite.

Symptoms of a blocked crown chakra include depression, greed, disassociation, a dominant personality, and destructive behavior. Physical symptoms include pituitary gland disorders, chronic fatigue, hair loss, and migraine. More serious manifestations may include brain tumors and cancer. There is a theory that a blocked crown chakra may also manifest in atheistic tendencies and the rejection of all that is spiritual and divine.

However, balancing the crown chakra is totally possible and important for keeping the other chakras aligned.

It is located on the very top of the head, and its color is violet.

Signs and Symptoms of a Blocked Chakra System

Obviously, a blockage in one or several chakras can affect their energy flow. It is essential to work on healing individual chakras that manifest the symptoms discussed previously, as they indicate a severe blockage or hyperactivity. But sometimes, the whole chakra system may just need a tune-up to rebalance and sync all of the chakras.

Symptoms may vary depending on which chakra needs particular attention, but the following are general warning signs that your chakras require attention.

- Difficulty expressing and articulating feelings.
- Personal and financial insecurity.
- Difficulty opening up in a relationship.
- Shoulder pain.
- Bad self-image.
- Low self-confidence.
- Digestive problems.
- Weight problems.
- Chronic fatigue.
- Fear of rejection.
- Excessive greed.
- Difficulty being assertive.
- Lymphatic issues.
- Depression.
- Hypersensitivity to light and sound.
- Hormonal issues.

- Feelings of isolation and loneliness.
- Excessive jealousy.
- Throat infections.
- Lack of motivation.
- Excessive pessimism and cynicism.

Balancing the Seven Chakras

If you recognize a symptom of an imbalanced chakra, it is a good idea to work on it as part of the overall awakening of the third eye. Here are some basic but effective steps for balancing each chakra:

Balancing the Root Chakra

- Achieve as much security as you can relating to your means of survival, such as saving for the future, paying bills on time, and ensuring that you have the basic necessities. This sounds pretty mundane but remember, this chakra is related to your earthly survival.

- The third eye meditations you have learned here will come in handy, because connecting to one of the spirit chakras will heal and balance the root chakra.

- Spending time in nature will also calm and open the root chakra, which is closely related to Mother Earth. Growing plants, gardening, picking wild berries, and other related activities are also recommended.

Balancing the Sacral Chakra

- Moderation is the key to balancing this chakra. A healthy diet and exercise routine are key to healing and balancing this chakra. Indulge and enjoy, but in moderation.

- Enjoy life through experiences by traveling, reading, taking creative classes, and going to art galleries. This helps balance the sacral chakra by connecting it to the finer enjoyments of life.

- Make the time to appreciate and spend time with loved ones.

Balancing the Solar Plexus Chakra

- This chakra is closely related to the third eye chakra in its associations. Therefore, balancing your third eye will have a positive effect on the solar plexus chakra. It will become empowered with the energy of wisdom and inner truth emanating from the third eye, causing it to also come into balance.

- If you have a tendency toward excessive talking or interrupting others, choose one day to listen to others and pause to choose your words when you do speak.

- Make a list of all the things you believe you are good at and create affirmations to foster your belief in yourself.

Balancing the Heart Chakra

- One of the symptoms of an unbalanced heart chakra is to be either too selfless or too selfish.

- If you spend too much time doing things for others, use some of that time to nurture and love yourself. Go out for a nice lunch with friends, spend the day at a spa, or simply take a warm bath with a few drops of chakra-healing essential oil. If you have a tendency to be a little selfish, practice going out of your way to be kind to others, smile at strangers on the street or give compliments to colleagues, but you must be sincere about it.

Balancing the Throat Chakra

- Practice expressing your emotions calmly and articulately.

- Be sincere to others; don't give fake compliments or tell white lies.

- Practice speaking clearly, even if it's with yourself.

Balancing the Crown Chakra

There is no specific way to balance this chakra, nor can it become overactive. This is because the powers associated with it are really too high to affect us as human beings. This chakra simply cannot be opened completely, although many passionate spiritualists have made this their life goal.

Having said that, you need to keep the crown chakra healthy by balancing the others and working on your spiritual development—such as opening the third eye.

You can work further on balancing the chakras by using the other methods discussed here, including meditation, affirmations, and the use of the associated crystals, colors, foods, and essential oils.

What to Expect

What you will experience once all of your chakras are aligned is nothing short of amazing. Here are some of the things you can expect:

- Feeling deeply relaxed.
- Having more energy.
- Having a calm mind, and being able to think more clearly.
- Feeling more optimistic about the future.
- A sense of expansion and openness.
- Reduced fear and anxiety.
- Improved mood.
- Improvement in aches and pains.
- Increase in insight.
- Better sleep.
- A feeling of being in harmony with life.

Basic Meditations for Balancing and Aligning the Chakras

These are two of the easiest and most common meditations to align the chakra system and quickly improve overall wellbeing.

Meditation 1

• Sit comfortably with your back straight. The lotus position with legs crossed is ideal for this meditation, but a comfortable straight-backed chair is fine as well. Make sure your legs are stretched out in a comfortable position.

• When you are completely comfortable, begin to breathe slowly, drawing the air as deeply as you can into your body.

• Focus completely on your breath and feel it moving slowly up your spine as you inhale, until it reaches the crown chakra. Feel it move back down your spine as you exhale.

• Repeat this part of the meditation twenty times.

• Now, you will stop and visualize each chakra. Start at the base of your spine and the root chakra and visualize its color (red).

• Visualize the energy flowing from your body into the root chakra and gradually filling it until it glows bright red.

• When you are ready, move up to the sacral chakra and visualize prana energy filling it until it glows with its associated color.

• Continue the meditation with each chakra and finish with the crown chakra.

• You may choose to end the meditation at this point or repeat the visualization, this time, moving down the spine and finishing with the root chakra.

• When you have finished, ground yourself with a few deep breaths.

Meditation 2

• Lie down in a quiet spot—whether it be on your bed, outside on the grass or anywhere else where you feel calm and peaceful.

• Breathe deeply for a few minutes, releasing all the tension and stress from your body.

- Set the intention, "I am now going to balance and align my chakras."

- Place one hand on the root chakra at the bottom of your spine and the other hand on the sacral chakra above it.

- Keep your hands resting on these two chakras until you feel that the energy between them has equalized. This may be a slight feeling of warmth or pulsation. If you feel nothing, don't worry. Just keep your hands on the two chakras until you feel ready to move on.

- Keeping one hand on the second chakra, move your hand up to the third chakra and repeat.

- Continue to move up the chakra system until you reach the crown chakra.

- Continue to lie there, and after a few minutes, you should experience a feeling of well-being and a slight energy shift in your body.

Conclusion

Your chakras all work together to equalize and integrate your physical, emotional, and spiritual health. Devoting some time to balance your chakras regularly is time well-spent. You will feel the effects of a balanced and aligned chakra system almost immediately.

Keeping your chakras balanced will keep you attuned to your inner self and increase your self-awareness. This is the real cornerstone of inner happiness and wellbeing.

Chapter Seven: How to Read Auras

Your third eye awakening will open the door to fascinating spiritual gifts. Be prepared to receive these gifts with gratitude and joy and use them wisely. One of these is the ability to see and read auras. This is a powerful gift to have if used correctly and with good intentions.

What Are Auras?

Every oxygen-breathing creature, including plants, has an aura. This has been the traditional belief, and now it has been scientifically proven.

An aura is non-physical magnetic energy, which emanates from a body and surrounds it in a sort of halo. Try rubbing your hands together vigorously for a few minutes and bringing your fingertips together. The slight spark of energy you feel is actually the energy of your aura. Just as it can be felt, an aura can also be seen.

Although the majority of people cannot see auras, there are those who can perceive them as a vivid field of energy surrounding the body. An aura does not move, but it can sometimes be seen subtly vibrating as if it is alive. A typical aura with all of its layers can extend several feet around the body. It actually has seven different layers that contain specific information.

The aura does not emanate from the physical body but is believed to be a form of cosmic energy that is released by what is known as the "subtle body."

The human aura can be described as a spiritual energy that reflects how a person is feeling physically and emotionally at a given moment.

The energy of an aura can affect and be affected by other people's auras. Have you ever sat or stood next to a stranger who exuded negative energy so that you felt drained and depressed? If you could read their aura, you would see that indeed, that person is in a state of anger or frustration and that their aura is affecting you. On the other hand, some people exude vibrant energy and optimism so that you want to be around them. This positive energy would also be reflected in their aura. In some spiritual circles, the term "energy vampire" is used to describe people who feed off of one's energy and leave them feeling negative and exhausted. These are the constant complainers, the constant criticizers, and the constant pessimists. As your spiritual awareness expands, you will learn to recognize this type of person by the way they make you feel. Reading their aura will also reflect these extremely negative qualities.

The energy of an aura can change from day to day, depending on a person's physical, mental, and spiritual state. The aura also reflects a person's character traits, which are more or less permanent. This can be read through the dominant color or layer of the aura.

Because the energy of auras is non-physical, the ability to see and read auras requires non-physical or clairvoyant gifts. The third eye awakening will, therefore, enable you to see auras.

The Seven Layers and Colors of an Aura

The first contour that appears in an aura appears as white or silver, with a milky opalescence. This first contour is not the aura itself but the energy that is being released by the aura. The first of the seven layers of the aura starts where this milky-white layer ends. The while or silvery "envelope" of the aura is usually the easiest and quickest to see when you begin training.

The seven layers are not equal in intensity and size. Each layer expands and contracts depending on one's spiritual, emotional, and physical health. Each layer contains information that can be "read."

Each aura layer corresponds to one of the seven chakras, which in turn relates to a specific energy. In fact, it is believed that the chakras themselves are the source of an aura's energy. Each layer of the aura also has a corresponding color, but as you will see, the color of an aura does not match the color of the chakra. The seven layers are:

Layer 1: The Etheric Aura

This corresponds to the root chakra. This layer contains information about the physical body. It reflects information about physical health. Its color is blue and various shades of blue.

Layer 2: The Emotional Aura

This corresponds to the sacral chakra, which relates to feelings and emotions. It provides information about blocks in this chakra; its color is usually a bright rainbow combination.

Layer 3: The Mental Aura

This corresponds to the solar plexus chakra and relates to thoughts, ideas, and knowledge. Its color is seen as bright shades of yellow.

Layer 4: The Astral Aura

This corresponds to the heart chakra, which reflects emotional and spiritual health. If the spiritual and emotional health is good, its colors will appear as a bright rainbow combination. If spiritual health is poor, its colors will appear faded and drab.

Layer 5: The Etheric Template Aura

This aura relates to information about the physical world and how we process information about our material surroundings. Its colors can vary.

Layer 6: The Celestial Aura

This corresponds to the third eye chakra and relates to the spiritual realm and spiritual gifts. Its colors are a combination of beautiful, incandescent pastels.

Layer 7: The Ketheric Aura

This corresponds to the crown chakra. It relates to universal cosmic energy and is the link to the divine. It reflects information about all the experiences of the soul that a person has been through. Its color appears as threads of shimmering gold.

In a healthy person, the aura can extend to a distance of several feet and will be very vibrant and vivid. In an unhealthy state, the contours of the aura are narrower, and its colors dull and faded.

This basic information will help you read auras—even your own—and understand where there may be a physical, spiritual, or emotional issue with yourself or with others.

What Science Tells Us about the Human Aura

There have been many claims made about capturing auras on film, and most of us have seen photos that apparently show this—though perhaps some of them are hoaxes as skeptics would argue. Although research in this field is somewhat rare, science has been able to confirm several facts about the nature of the human aura.

At Tokyo University, a group of scientists ran a series of experiments, where they were able to capture auras with the use of ultra-sensitive cameras. The conclusion? Auras are real and do exist.

The study also found that the auras of the participant were most visible in the area of the face, especially around the cheeks, nose, mouth, and neck. (This is where you might want to focus when you start reading auras).

Although research is ongoing, the potential findings could be groundbreaking. Scientists think that glowing areas in certain parts of the body could indicate a disorder or disease, which would make aura reading a revolutionary diagnostic tool.

It is ironic that there is still debate about whether auras really exist, given that Ancient Eastern medicine has long understood the role of auras and chakras in healing. In fact, the ancient healing traditions brilliantly understood that by dealing with the corresponding problematic chakra, it is possible to target the root cause of an illness rather than just treat its symptoms. Unfortunately, modern medicine tends to do the opposite, where, in many cases, the symptoms are alleviated while the underlying cause is left untreated. Today, holistic treatments like acupuncture, facial and foot reflex therapy, and Reiki rely on these ancient methods of finding and healing the root cause through the chakra system.

Russian scientist Dr Konstantin Korotkov from the University of St. Petersburg is conducting some fascinating and unique studies on the relation of human thoughts and energy (auras) on the surrounding environment. He is noted for his work titled *Aura and Consciousness: New Stage of Scientific Understanding*. His research is exploring how the energy of our aura can extend to the environment and affect the people and other living things around us.

Suffice it to say that research in this field is ongoing and the future looks promising. Science is finally acknowledging that the unseen spiritual realm may hold immense potential and benefit for humankind.

Why Learn to Read Auras?

Reading an aura means that you are actually reading the vibration of the energy released from the matter underneath it. In other words, a problematic aura may point to a problem in the area of the body that it corresponds to.

On a personal level, reading auras can benefit almost every area of your life, whether social, professional, or personal. It will also enable you to help others in the following ways:

• When you are able to analyze someone's energy it can help you to understand whether they are nervous, distressed, angry, or calm—and be able to adjust your reactions accordingly. For example, if you sense that a person is distressed or sad, you don't want to add pressure by being demanding or critical. If a person is angry, you can avoid triggering their anger. If you sense a problem in someone you are close to, lending a sympathetic ear can help. It is a little bit like being able to read minds.

• Understanding why people are behaving in a certain way will allow you to be more tolerant and understanding toward them. This will enormously improve your relationships on all levels—and make you very popular as well!

• You can also reach out to people whom you feel are struggling with certain issues and suggest to them where the problem lies (from the color of the aura or its corresponding chakra). You can advise them to seek medical or psychiatric help if necessary.

• Reading your own aura can help you establish priorities in your life, such as going on vacation, going for a checkup, increasing certain foods in your diet, or making more time to nurture family relationships.

• Reading your own aura can help you make better choices, such as ending an unhealthy relationship or changing careers.

• It can help you to take better care of yourself.

• It can improve personal relationships with family and friends.

• You can improve finances by finding and treating imbalances in areas of abundance and gratitude.

• You will strengthen your sense of purpose.

• It helps you to release painful experiences from your past.

- It helps you to develop and grow your other psychic gifts.

- It can help you to release the feelings that you are overwhelmed and powerless.

Basic Exercises to Help you Read Auras

Learning how to see and read auras is pretty easy for most people, although it does require practice. You can very quickly train yourself to see the first layer of an aura (usually a pale shade of blue) around people, plants, and even animals—yes, you can read your pet's aura too!

However, being able to see and read the other six aura layers requires a bit more serious practice and may take longer.

You should have no trouble becoming very skilled at this practice once your third eye chakra is awakened and empowered.

Start training with these basic exercises before you attempt the real thing:

Exercise 1: Seeing Your Own Aura

- Stand before a large mirror. It does not necessarily have to be full-length, but at least one that reflects the full upper half of your body. Note: The room you choose must have neutral walls.

- Ideally, you should be nude, but if you choose not to be, wear white, beige, or light gray clothing.

- Look in the mirror and focus your peripheral vision on a point slightly above your shoulder. If you focus intently enough, you will be able to see the etheric aura around your head and even around your neck.

- Continue to gaze at the energy in your peripheral vision for as long as you like.

- If you lose the focus of your peripheral vision, start the exercise again until the aura reappears.

Exercise 2: Seeing Pranic Energy in the Sky

This is an excellent exercise for training the peripheral vision and strengthening concentration.

- This exercise is done outside at a time when the sun is not too bright, or on a cloudy day.

- Sit or lie down in a comfortable position and allow your body a few moments to relax.

- Look up at the sky and let your gaze drift off into the distance without allowing your eyes to focus on any specific point.

- Continue to just gaze without focusing for one or two minutes.

- Next, bring your focus to your peripheral vision.

- You should be able to see black and white spots floating around in the sky.

- While still focusing on your peripheral vision, follow one of the moving dots.

- Continue to track the separate moving dot for as long as you choose.

- Skeptics claim that this is actually an optical illusion, but there is no concrete evidence to prove this. In any case, it is good training for the peripheral vision.

How to See Another Person's Aura

Start simple. Human auras are much more complex than other living things. A great suggestion is to start simple with a small plant in your home.

- Sit in a comfortable position with the plant in front of you and a neutral background behind it. The light in the room should not be too bright.

- Gaze at a point about ten centimeters above the plant. Try not to let your eyes go out of focus.

- Direct the vision of your third eye to the plant: feel it expanding into surrounding the whole plant as you continue to gaze at it without shifting your focus.

- The aura of the plant will begin to appear.

Note: Plant auras do not contain colors because plants lack the physical and emotional complexities of humans. The aura will simply appear as a faint glow without colors.

Practice this exercise with different-sized plants until it becomes easy to focus and see their auras.

Practice on yourself. Practice on yourself with the mirror exercise described in the last section. The first step is to get good at seeing the first layer of your aura, as in the exercise. This will be a faint colorless glow that surrounds your head and body. This will always be the easiest layer to see.

The next step is to begin perceiving the other layers of your aura. Extend your focus outwards and continue to gaze intently until you are also able to see the other layers of your aura.

This more difficult step requires dedicated practice and intent. The more you practice, the easier it will become to perceive your own aura, and the more vivid the different layers will appear.

Practice on family members and friends. When you feel you are skilled enough, start practicing on other people, starting with a family member or friend. Have the person sit in front of you and repeat the same steps you did for seeing your own aura, except this time you gaze at a spot above the other person's shoulder. You should be able to perceive their aura.

Important Tips

- Do not expect to become a pro overnight. While some people are able to learn how to see auras more quickly than others, the norm is that this process takes time and practice. Don't get discouraged, and keep your intent strong.

- Do not expect to see aura colors right away. Again, this requires many hours of practice. However, the first time you are able to perceive that initial faint glow around another person's body, be sure that you are making progress.

- Try not to blink as this will completely "reset" your focus when you are a beginner. Over time, you will be able to continue seeing the aura no matter how many times you blink.

Background and Lighting

Some beginners find it easier to see auras in a darkened room, so play around with lighting to see what works best for you. Also, having your subjects sit in front of a white or black background usually makes it easier to see their auras.

Ask People before Reading Their Auras

Never read a person's aura without asking their permission first. Some people may feel uncomfortable with the idea and decline, while others may find the idea fascinating. Reading someone's aura is an invasion of their privacy, so it is only ethical that you ask their permission first.

Meditate Often on Your Third Eye

Remember, clairvoyance is a new and amazing gift that you are discovering within yourself. Not only does it require practice and patience, but also that you keep your third eye nurtured and in optimal health.

Reading Auras and the Meanings of Colors

When you become skilled at seeing auras, you will be able to see the different layers: but sometimes, one color will be more dominant or vivid than the others. Learning to understand what each color means can tell you a lot about the person's overall health and wellbeing.

This dominant color also reflects an individual's personality and can in some cases reflect their future destiny.

Red Aura

People who have red as the dominant color in their aura are known for being adventurous and always eager to try new things and engage in new experiences. They are the type of people who will try anything at least once. They are energetic and live life to the fullest. They are direct, very opinionated, and can be brutally honest at times.

Red-aura people are physically and mentally strong and are less prone to illness and fatigue. They excel in athletics and sports.

The downside of a person with a red aura is that they may sometimes live too much in the fast lane, causing them to burn themselves out or get into trouble. They are also prone to outbursts of anger and jealousy and sometimes even violent outbursts.

The adventurous spirit of the red-aura individual makes them feel bored rather quickly, which could put a strain on their personal relationships and professional lives. Their extreme competitiveness and desire to be number one may also cause them to be insensitive and selfish at times.

Pink Aura

A pink aura represents love, selflessness, and giving. People who have a dominant pink aura put love and friendship above everything else. They love being amidst family and friends at all times; giving and receiving love. They are very romantic, and their relationships with partners and spouses tend to be for life.

Pink-aura people are also very health conscious and look after themselves well with a healthy diet and exercise. Their deep health-consciousness makes them very attuned to other people's health needs, and they make brilliant doctors and healers. They are also very passionate about social justice and human rights and tend to be advocates for good causes.

The only downside is that their overly loving and giving nature may cause these people to be taken advantage of.

Yellow Aura

People with a predominantly yellow aura are very rational, logical, and analytical—and amazingly intelligent. They excel in science and mathematics and are great in careers that require analytical thinking. They are extremely articulate and know how to communicate their thoughts brilliantly.

The downside of this color is the tendency to become a workaholic and to put work and career above personal relationships. This type of person is also more prone to mental issues such as depression and isolation because they don't give priority to social and personal relationships.

Orange Aura

Fun-loving, humorous, and social, are the traits that best describe a person with a dominant orange aura. They are very giving and generous and love socializing with friends and being the center of attention. Their natural honesty, kind-heartedness, and empathy make them very popular and well-liked. They are much attuned to the emotions of others and are great listeners and sympathizers. This is the person people go to when they want to pour out their hearts.

The downsides are that an orange-aura person can be stubborn and quick to lose their temper; however, they do not carry grudges and are very quick to apologize, forgive, and make things right.

Green Aura

A predominantly green aura reflects a highly creative personality that strives for perfection. At the same time, this person is very hard-working, down to earth, and realistic. They think carefully and seldom make rash decisions. This is indeed a great combination! That is why green-aura people can be highly successful in business.

This type of personality is also health-conscious, and while they love food, they are always careful to follow a balanced and nutritious diet. They love communing with nature and enjoy any outdoor activity.

The only downside is when these people put their creativity before the more practical things in life.

Blue Aura

The main personality trait of an individual with a blue aura is a very strong and sometimes dominant character. These people are highly charismatic, brilliant communicators, and eloquent speakers. They are intuitive and organized and have the capacity to become great leaders.

The downside of this color is the tendency for overwork and burnout.

Brown Aura

This aura usually appears as a shade of light brown and indicates distress, confusion, or anguish. This person is going through some major issues in their life or is simply having trouble finding their purpose.

On the other hand, a dark brown aura indicates selfishness, deception, and a tendency to look for fault in others.

Purple Aura

A dominant purple aura is an indication of psychic qualities. This person is often seen as the dark, silent, mysterious type and is very sensitive to the moods and vibrations of others.

This person has a passion for learning and has a very philosophical, intuitive, and inquisitive mind. This person is not very social, nor do they have a large number of friends. But they are very loyal, and the friendships they do make are life-lasting and strong. A purple aura person also loves animals and nature.

The downside is that this person's over-sensitivity to the emotions and moods of others can cause them to feel sapped and drained of energy when the negative vibrations of others overwhelm them.

Gold Aura

A gold aura indicates a very artistic person with an eye for beauty. They love to wear beautiful clothes and jewelry and surround themselves with luxuries and uniquely beautiful items. It is not surprising that they also love being the center of attention.

On the downside, a gold aura person does not take criticism well, even if it is well-meant. There may also be a tendency to overspend on luxuries and the finer things in life.

Silver Aura

This aura can either appear as silver, white, or silvery-white and is the sign of a gifted and talented person. This person is very intuitive and psychic and is easily able to access these gifts. This, combined with their high intelligence, allows them to make very successful life choices. They have an almost magnetic attraction for others, and yet they are very careful about choosing their circle of friends.

The only downside is when this type of person neglects to use their special gifts or uses them in the wrong way.

Black Aura

This aura has very negative implications. It may indicate a serious illness, so it is highly advisable that this person goes for an immediate physical examination. A black aura also indicates hatred, envy, and depression.

Conclusion

Seeing and reading auras is both an art and an acquired skill. When you practice constantly, you will become quite adept at seeing auras and their different colors. It becomes an art when you are able to distinguish the dominant colors of auras and their implications. Of course, it goes without saying that the more you awaken and nurture your third eye chakra, the more you will become a master aura reader.

Chapter Eight: Psychic Visions and Clairvoyance

An awakened third eye chakra that is healthy and balanced opens the door to pure perception and inner seeing. As we have learned in the last chapter, this pure vision allows you to access your higher consciousness. It is through higher consciousness that you are able to transcend the physical realm and enjoy the spiritual gifts of aura reading, psychic visions, and clairvoyance. It is important to understand that while keeping the whole chakra system balanced is important, these spiritual gifts can only be accessed through the continuous nurturing and interaction with your inner eye.

Psychic Visions vs. Clairvoyance

It is difficult to identify the specific difference between psychic visions and clairvoyance. However, they are both parts of the spectrum of psychic abilities one can develop. Psychic visions are a form of clairvoyance where you receive information about something that will happen in the future. Clairvoyance can take the form of psychic visions as well as information you receive about people or events through intuition or by reading auras. A highly developed clairvoyant sense can also allow you to receive messages and information by perceiving the energy of a certain person, thing, or place.

Let's just say that both are amazing gifts to have and that both are a form of extra-sensory perception (ESP).

What Is a Psychic Vision?

A psychic experience or vision is an insight that is so vivid, intense, and clear that it often seems more realistic—and more rational—than real life. There is really no better way to describe it. You simply must experience it yourself in order to understand this somewhat vague definition. To follow are the basic characteristics of a psychic vision:

- A psychic vision is also called "an illumination."

- It may be brought on by an emergency, either emotional or physical.

- Psychic visions can occur in a sleep state as dreams, when you are awake, or while you are meditating.

- A psychic vision may take the form of a "movie" that either runs before your closed eyes or in your mind—in this case, in your third eye.

- You might see lights or auras in your peripheral vision, or a person's aura may become apparent when you were not trying to see it. Listen to what your intuition tells you about the colors.

- Clear dreams during sleep where you are in control of what happens or where you know what will happen.

- Psychic visions give you information that you cannot access through your other senses. They are basically your intuition communicating with you.

What Do Psychic Visions Mean?

Some psychic visions will have immediate relevance for you, so that you will be able to understand their meaning right away. Other visions may be more confusing or may have no relevance at all.

The first way to interpret a psychic dream is to use your intuition to try and understand its meaning. The second method is to practice the following meditation:

- Sit or lie down comfortably, breathe deeply to relax and bring your focus to your third eye.

- Ask your third eye to inform you of what the vision means.

- Wait for the answer, and if nothing comes to you, continue to ask and wait.

- You should receive a message in due time, but if not, end the meditation. You may receive a message later in the day or even a few days later.

Psychic visions can be a wonderful gift of love to someone who needs guidance in their life. A psychic dream may actually be able to help someone find their true purpose and the fulfillment of their destiny. Psychic visions may also be useful for yourself and others in avoiding or averting danger.

On the downside, psychic visions can be extremely distressing to your emotional health, such as when you receive information about a person's death. It is important to stress here that nobody has ever been able—or will ever be able—to foresee or predict another person's death conclusively. This is something that only God / the Creator/ the universe knows.

In most cases, the vision will symbolize a serious illness or some harm coming to the person in question. In any case, these types of visions are truly dreaded. Be prepared to receive them but never act upon them by telling someone that they are going to die. You must either ignore them and hope for the best or wait and see if you will receive further messages that will clarify the meaning of that initial vision.

What is Clairvoyance?

Clairvoyance literally means "clear seeing." This refers to psychic dreams, visions, intuitive messages, and other forms of insight or wisdom that you receive from your third eye. Sometimes, these moments of clear seeing will be brief and undramatic, while at other times, they will appear in vivid psychic visions.

Sometimes they might come in a strong premonition about something or someone, such as you suddenly thinking of a person you haven't seen for years and then bumping into them the next day.

This the closest definition of clairvoyance; again, to fully understand it, you must experience it for yourself and allow your third eye to guide you in interpreting the messages.

The basic characteristics of clairvoyance are as follows:

• Psychic flashes: these may be colors, dancing lights or floating dots, or the sudden appearance of a face.

• When you feel like it, you will find it very easy to daydream and ignore any disruptions around you. You may or may not have psychic insights during these daydreams.

• You will be able to see in your third eye how things fit together. In many areas of your life, you will start getting glimpses of how parts of the greater puzzle come together. The resulting wisdom you will gain from this is simply breathtaking.

• You may find that your sense of direction is amazingly spot-on at certain times. This could very well be your clairvoyance coming into play.

• You may receive messages through clairaudience (psychic hearing) or clairsentience (psychic feelings) or through psychic knowing (clairvoyance) where you intuitively just know that something is true or that something will happen.

- You may receive visions of how to plan for certain events in your life by seeing them play out in your mind.

Exercises to Develop Psychic and Clairvoyant Abilities

Keeping your third eye open and balanced is really the best way to access these spiritual gifts. Bear in mind that there is no guaranteed method to make yourself become clairvoyant or have psychic visions. Some people will experience these gifts more frequently, while for others, these experiences will be rare. However, there are a few ways to help you develop your higher consciousness in order to develop your spiritual powers further.

Meditation. All of the meditations and exercises discussed in this book should be regularly practiced. This is by far the best method to develop your spiritual gifts. In addition, practice this meditation as well:

- Sit or lie down comfortably. Breathe deeply until your whole body feels loose and relaxed.

- Close your eyes and visualize the spot at the back of your forehead that is right in front of your third eye. Visualize this spot as a black movie screen.

- Focus on this screen with your third eye.

- Wait and see what appears on the screen.

- Continue the meditation for ten minutes.

- You may not have a vivid vision or see anything clearly, but you may receive a psychic flash or a spark of intuition.

Crystals that promote clairvoyance. Certain crystals and stones can be used during meditation to clear the mind, allowing psychic energy to filter through. These include cherry opal and aquamarine, emerald, and yellow labradorite. They can be easily purchased online. Place one of these stones on your third eye as you meditate lying down.

Visualization Exercises

Practice visualization as much as possible, every day, for a few minutes. It is one of the easiest but most effective ways to develop clairvoyance and exercise the third eye. The best way to develop your special gift is by learning to see images with your third eye as clearly as possible.

Visualization Exercise 1: Your Perfect Place

• Sit or lie in a relaxed position and visualize yourself in your dream location. This place doesn't necessarily have to be somewhere you have been. It could be a beautiful deserted island, a quiet beach, a green valley filled with wildflowers ... et cetera.

• Visualize every minute detail in your third eye until you can actually feel yourself there. For example, you are able to see and smell the wildflowers around you; or feel the warm waves lapping at your feet. Visualize each minute detail, color, sound, and smell until you feel transported to that place.

Visualization Exercise 2: Objects and Symbols

Visualize any object or symbol of your choice with your third eye until you are able to see it clearly in your mind's eye, in as much detail as possible. You can also visualize faces, as well.

Visualization Exercise 3: Visualize Your Artwork

• Write your name on a white piece of paper and use colored markers and glitter to highlight and decorate the letters. Use vibrant colors and designs.

• When you are finished, gaze at your artwork for about a minute, then close your eyes and visualize it with your third eye, recalling as many of the colors and details as you can, as if you see it with your physical eyes.

Visualization Exercise 4: The Flowers Exercise

• Prepare a small bunch of beautiful flowers in different types and colors.

- Spend a few minutes gently touching the flowers, noticing the different shapes, colors, textures, and smells. Take all the time you need to explore the flowers with your senses.

- Put the flowers down, close your eyes, and take a few deep breaths.

- Focus on your third eye and visualize the bunch of flowers resting within your third eye. Try to recall every detail of color and texture, and "feel" their fragrance.

- Wait and see if any visions, symbols, or other messages come up. If not, that's fine. Just continue to practice the exercise regularly.

- This exercise can also be practiced by focusing on and visualizing one flower at a time.

Note: You can do the exercise with leaves, fresh herbs, or even a pinecone. The goal of using earthy objects is to help keep you grounded. This is very important for beginners.

Visualization Exercise 5: Memory Games

These are a fun way to engage your third eye and hone your perception. There are dozens of enjoyable memory games that you can play online, or you can try the following:

Missing item. Enlist the help of a family member or friend for this one. Have them remove one item from your bedroom, kitchen, or bathroom as you wait in another room.

- Walk into the room and try to discover what item was removed.

Rearranged item. Layout several items on a table and take a few moments to stare at them and remember how they are arranged.

- Close your eyes, and have your friend rearrange one item. Open your eyes and try to see which item was moved.

Conclusion

Accessing your psychic abilities is a two-fold effort. You should practice doing it in a structured way by regularly practicing the exercises described here. This is where you intentionally disconnect yourself from the distractions of the outside world and make time to work on developing your gifts in calm, quiet surroundings. You may or may not have psychic experiences during your practice sessions, but know that you are laying down a strong foundation for cultivating these abilities.

Secondly, you must be open and alert to psychic experiences in your daily life.

Finally, learn to fully trust your third eye and the messages it gives you. It is natural that you will struggle with disbelief and skepticism at first. You may ignore subtle messages and tell yourself that your subconscious mind is playing tricks on you. But the more you experience these psychic gifts, the more you will learn to trust, embrace, and look forward to them. The fact that you are able to access a realm that transcends the physical world takes some time to sink in!

Your goal is to allow your psychic gifts to become second nature and a wonderful source of enrichment to your life. A word of warning: using your gifts to feel powerful and "omnipotent" should never be your goal. Use them to empower and enrich yourself spiritually as well as to empower and guide others.

Chapter Nine: General Tips and Recommendations

Keeping your third eye chakra balanced and healthy is an ongoing process, but hopefully, after you get a glimpse of what third eye awakening can do in your life, you will be motivated to make it a life-long labor of love.

The tips and recommendations in this chapter can be useful additions to your third eye awakening toolkit. Some of them may be part of your lifestyle already, which is great.

Small Lifestyle Changes That Will Make the Exercises More Effective

Sleep in complete darkness. Given the strong interconnection between your third eye and the pineal gland, it makes sense to ensure that the pineal gland is decalcified and working properly.

The pineal gland starts releasing melatonin when darkness sets in, preparing you for sleep. Melatonin is vital for a balanced circadian rhythm and quality sleep, which is important for clarity, focus, and a healthy third eye.

Daylight and artificial light can disrupt melatonin production and throw your sleep-wake cycle off balance. Sleep in a completely darkened room, if possible. If you find this too uncomfortable, a small amber nightlight is fine.

If you happen to work nights and sleep during the day, invest in good-quality blackout curtains that prevent any light from filtering in.

Create a personal meditation space. Meditation is such a vital part of your new routine that it makes sense to designate a special place for it.

This could be an unused room in your home or a screened off corner of your bedroom. This will become your calm, welcoming meditation haven. Make your space as relaxing as possible with a thick rug, meditation mat, or comfortable chair. Lay out your crystals and stones in bowls on a low table, as well as candles, and an essential oil diffuser. Place cushions on the floor, display one or two beautiful items that you love, and consider a beautiful and serene wall hanging or poster.

Let your creativity and intuition guide you as to what you need to instantly feel calm and relaxed when you step into your personal meditation space.

Reduce your exposure to blue light. Blue light is toxic to the pineal gland, so avoid it like the plague! Ban fluorescent lighting from your home and use amber-based lighting throughout the home.

More importantly, limit your exposure to blue light from digital screens like cell phones, TV screens, and computer monitors. If you spend hours in front of a computer, install a blue light blocking screen. These screens are also available for cell phones.

This applies specifically to your bedroom. Remove all digital screens from the bedroom.

Fasting for third-eye health. The higher chakras (the heart chakra and upwards) are less related to physical functions and have more to do with mental states and spirituality. Fasting for a few hours can actually energize and balance these chakras, including the third eye.

Consider fasting from morning till noon every once in a while and break your fast with a light, nutritious meal.

Try sensory deprivation. This one is a little bit extreme, but perhaps the more adventurous reader may consider trying it out! Float tanks or deprivation tanks offer the experience of being totally immersed in a dark tank of water so that you become entirely separated from your senses.

A flat tank experience enhances your third eye awareness and heightens extrasensory perception.

Drink herbal tea. Herbal teas such as bilberry, eyebright, juniper, and anise keep your pineal gland balanced and decalcified; plus, they have stress-reducing properties to help you better focus on your exercises and meditation. Try these herbal teas for a delicious hot or cold beverage that will invigorate and balance your third eye chakra:

• Eyebright heightens intuition and increases inspiration, allowing you to have more consistent inner thoughts and insights.

• Ginkgo promotes blood circulation and oxygenation of the brain, allowing you to remember your dreams and giving you more mental clarity to interpret them.

• Black raspberry contains calming and purifying qualities that bring clarity to your third eye.

• Amaranth is ideal for developing your psychic gifts as it raises the vibration of the third eye chakra.

• Blueberry tea raises inner eye awareness.

• Bilberry tea raises third eye awareness and is also beneficial to eyesight.

Try different combinations to create your own personalized brew, or drink them individually.

Create essential oil blends. Blend a combination of the essential oils discussed earlier and add them to your beauty products such as shampoo, lotion, conditioner, and hand cream.

Exercise daily. Even if it is just a brisk walk around the block, fifteen minutes of daily exercise is the perfect way to keep your whole body healthy and your chakras balanced.

Take supplements. The following supplements are especially beneficial to the health of the pineal gland and your third eye chakra:

- Cod liver oil is a natural supplement packed with vitamin A, which helps maintain pineal gland health and keep it decalcified.

- Vitamin K helps decalcify soft tissues, including the pineal gland.

- Neem extract has been used since ancient times to boost immune system health and detoxify the body. It can be purchased in health food stores.

Reduce Stress. Keep yourself and your third eye calm and grounded by eliminating stress factors in your daily life. Take stock of your normal day and identify the things that stress you out. Try to reduce or eliminate these stress factors by rescheduling certain tasks, adding more structure to your family routine, or delegating work at the office.

Make mindfulness a mindset. Living in the past or constantly thinking about the future (both of which are out of our hands to change) can be the biggest obstacle to third eye awakening. Living in the present moment, with total mindfulness, keeps the mind and intuition open and ready to accept all that comes to us in a neutral, non-judgmental way. Adopting a mindful mindset helps you to avoid negative thoughts and feelings that cloud your perception and block the inner eye chakra.

Do not allow yourself to fall into a pattern of ruminating about the past and wondering how things would have gone if you had done things differently. This highly negative pattern of thought is harmful to spiritual awakening. Likewise, fretting and overthinking about the future is equally negative.

Here are three additional exercises to cultivate mindfulness:

Exercise 1: Mindful Immersion

This exercise helps to promote contentment and tranquility in the present moment.

- Choose a mundane task that you normally try to get through as fast as possible, and where your thoughts are usually focused on something else. This could be doing laundry, tidying a room, or folding clothes. Let's take washing dishes as an example.

- As you fill the sink with water and washing liquid, focus on every detail. Hear the sound of water gushing into the sink, notice the color and smell of the washing liquid, focus on the bubbles forming in the water.

- Wash and rinse the dishes, becoming totally immersed in the color and feel of each item in your hand, the sound of the sponge or scrubber as you are cleaning, and the rush of the water over your hand as you rinse each item.

- The goal is to immerse yourself fully during every step that you normally do, as if experiencing it for the first time.

- Dismiss any disruptive thoughts and bring your focus gently back to what you are doing.

Exercise 2: Mindful Listening

The aim of this exercise is to help you totally immerse yourself in the present moment without allowing judgment to cloud your perception.

- Choose a song or a musical piece that you have never heard before. Don't allow your judgment of the title or genre to interfere with your choice.

- Close your eyes and listen to the song.

- Immerse yourself in the music, and just let yourself be carried away. Immediately dismiss any judgmental thoughts about whether you like the music, the voice, the beat, etc.

- Next, begin to focus and explore the sound of each instrument, the melodies, solo voices, et cetera. Again, do this with a completely open mind and do not make judgments.

This is an amazing exercise to keep you grounded and heighten your senses.

Exercise 3: Mindful Appreciation

The goal of this exercise is to promote gratitude and appreciation of things or people that we take for granted. Gratitude is a wonderful source of nourishment for the third eye chakra and for spiritual development in general.

- Take the time each day to notice and give thanks for several things that add value to your life.

- For example, when reading a book, stop to be thankful for the paper, the printing press, and the author, which all made it possible for you to enjoy the book. You can do the same with your computer, cell phone, and even when flicking on a light switch.

- Take the time to appreciate and be thankful for your wonderful family and supportive friends or even a helpful shop assistant.

- Keeping your heart filled with gratitude and love will promote feelings of harmony with the world and keep your third eye lucid and aware.

Consider Minimalism

As your third eye becomes awakened, and you begin to experience inner knowing and wisdom, one of the first things you will understand is that there is much, much more to life than material possessions. You will no longer be interested in buying the latest gadget or wearing the latest fashion. A bigger house or a better car no longer become priorities that you spend sleepless nights thinking about. Keeping up with the Joneses? You will laugh at the idea. The triviality of what you once thought was so important will hit you in the face. As a result, you may naturally find yourself gravitating toward a more minimalist lifestyle.

What is Minimalism?

Becoming a minimalist means simplifying your life by living with the bare essentials. What is considered as the "bare essentials" differs from one person to another. Basically, it means decluttering your space and adopting the mindset that more is less. Minimalists train themselves to control their consumption and materialistic tendencies—which is not easy in our modern world.

Minimalism, unlike many people imagine, does not mean living frugality and depriving yourself. The keyword is simplification; you can simplify and streamline your lifestyle and live like a king—but with much more peace of mind and more time and money to enjoy the things that really matter in life.

Many minimalists report that this way of living has completely changed their outlook as well as their priorities. Some of the many benefits of minimalism include:

- Mental clarity. Decluttering your home or office will literally declutter your mind. There is a strong relationship between material possessions and mental and emotional health. Decluttering your home will actually make you feel more peaceful and in control of your life.

- Better finances. By living with less and buying less, you will be able to save money—quite a lot, actually. This is great for balancing those lower chakras, especially the root chakra, which is the cause of our financial insecurity and fear.

- More freedom. Breaking the bonds of materialism brings a tremendous sense of liberation, joy, and tranquility. You have the freedom and time to pursue the things that are truly valuable in life, such as traveling, enriching your mind, and spending time with the people you love.

Basic Steps to Simplify Your Life

Start with one room. Start with a clean slate by thoroughly decluttering one room in your house. Remove everything you don't use on a regular basis: including items in drawers and on shelves. Reorganize the room so that it is streamlined and open. Add a few touches of color if you want. Explore how you feel about the new space. Add or remove items until you feel that the space is welcoming and peaceful. Repeat the process with every room in your house until everything is streamlined, simple, and tidy.

Store or donate. Store things that hold dear memories for you and donate clothes, furniture, and other items that you don't use regularly.

Invest in good quality items. When you need to buy something, always make sure it is top quality. Good quality items are made to last, require less maintenance, and show less wear and tear over time. This goes for clothes as well.

Apply the 60-90 day rule. Get rid of anything you haven't used in 60 to 90 days. It is as simple as that. Store these items if you feel you may need them in the future, but if not, get rid of them.

Declutter your time. This means learning to say "no" to tasks and engagements and people that you feel are an unreasonable demand on your time. It means prioritizing tasks and delegating as much as you can. It also means phasing out relationships that drain you emotionally or that just aren't going anywhere.

Minimalism can be beneficial for peace of mind and spiritual calm. It is worth giving it a try.

Confront and release painful memories and experiences. The negative feelings that we bury deep inside of us are very detrimental to our spiritual development. Unless you are honestly able to confront and release painful memories and experiences, it will be very difficult to harmonize and balance the chakra system.

There are dozens of guided meditations online designed for this purpose. Consider downloading a couple of them and working on releasing your negative energy.

You may want to consider therapy if you are carrying severe mental scars that require more in depth probing in order to heal. Awakening the third eye chakra and developing psychic gifts will not automatically resolve such emotional issues.

Invest in a meditation app. Meditation apps offer a wide variety of guided meditations, nature sounds, and binaural beat tracks, and even mantras and chants. Many of them contain features for scheduling meditation, as well as alerts and reminders. They are useful for having with you to meditate outdoors or when you are traveling. Meditation apps come in a wide variety, are fairly inexpensive and are readily available online. Just Google "meditation apps" or "third eye chakra meditation apps."

Join a like-minded community. Take advantage of the positive side of social media by joining a community or group of like-minded people. If you are lucky enough to find one in your area, these groups often hold meetups and invite guest speakers and sometimes arrange retreats.

Joining an online community will empower and reinforce your spiritual journey. You can exchange advice, share ideas, find plenty of support, and even make some good friends.

Check-in with yourself regularly and reflect on your thoughts and actions. This is an important skill to cultivate because it enhances self-awareness. Stop and reflect on what you are doing or saying at certain points in the day. Are you mindful? Has your mind strayed into negative thoughts? Are you really listening to the person talking to you? Are you allowing your judgment to fog your clarity of thinking?

Observing your thoughts and analyzing them in this way will keep you mindful and grounded throughout the day.

Keep your intention strong. Working with spiritual energy requires a clear and strong intention. Before meditating or practicing an exercise, always remember to state your intention so that your mind registers it and retains it.

An intention may be general, such as "healing the third eye" or more specific, such as "seeing this person's aura" or "visualizing this flower." Affirmations are some of the best ways to keep your intentions strong and focused throughout the day.

Conclusion

The rewards of maintaining a healthy third eye chakra with these additional methods are well worth the effort. Experiment with the methods discussed in this chapter, one or two at a time, adding them to your regular meditation routine. How many you choose to practice is totally up to you.

The result will be higher self-awareness, more confidence in yourself, more vivid and frequent dreams and psychic experiences, and more inner peace, as you learn to trust your third eye intuition.

Chapter Ten: Putting It All Together

This may seem like a lot of information to take in and apply in your already too-busy life. Understandably, you may be feeling overwhelmed. Where do you start? How often should you practice? How do you incorporate the exercises and techniques to form a personalized plan? This chapter will answer all your questions.

Schedule the Priorities

There are three main activities that you should schedule on a daily or weekly basis.

1. Third eye chakra meditation. Ideally, you should meditate at least once a day for at least fifteen minutes. Twice or thrice a day would be even better. A good idea is to do a short daily meditation and schedule time for longer sessions (30 minutes at least) on weekends and days off.

2. Visualization exercises. Once a day is good but as your third eye becomes stronger, you will be able to visualize faster and may have more time in the day to fit in more than one visualization.

3. Mindfulness exercises. Mindfulness is the key to keeping yourself grounded throughout the day, and maintaining third eye clarity. As we have seen, mindfulness exercises such as the "mindful immersion" exercise, can be done anytime and in any place. Simply sitting down at your desk and turning on your computer can be an opportunity for mindful immersion or mindful gratitude. You should be able to engage in more than one mindful practice during your day.

This is your starting point. Depending on your individual work and family schedule, use a red pen or marker to make a weekly schedule with the above three activities blocked into your day. These are your priorities. Anyone can make time for priorities, even if it means waking up half an hour earlier each day or limiting TV time in the evening. Just set the intention to stick to your schedule.

Make These Priorities a Lifestyle

Just as exercise and diet are part of your lifestyle, enjoying and cultivating the spiritual benefits of an awakened third eye chakra should also become a regular part of your lifestyle. The more you meditate, visualize, and practice mindfulness, the more naturally these will come to you until they become part of your daily routine. In fact, they will become welcome opportunities for relaxation and inner peace, especially in times of hardship or crisis.

Simple Tips for Making Time to Meditate

Get up earlier. Experts say that the best time to meditate is early in the morning. Getting up half an hour or fifteen minutes earlier each day will allow you to start your day with meditation. If you are just not a morning person, try getting up five minutes earlier and gradually increase the time.

The important thing is that you meditate as soon as you get up. Use the bathroom if you need to sit down, and meditate immediately. This so you don't waste time pottering around and doing other stuff like checking email or brushing your teeth. Do that after you finish meditating.

Lunch breaks. Rather than going out to lunch, bring your own lunch to the office or send someone out for a quick bite. Close the door, find a relaxing spot, and meditate for fifteen or twenty minutes. Better yet, if there is a park nearby and the weather is suitable, enjoy your meditation session outdoors. This will also do wonders for your focus and productivity.

Commuting. Commuting on a bus or train may not be the best environment for meditating, but it is a great opportunity for mindful exercises and visualization.

When you feel stress setting in. When the stress hormone is triggered in your body, it wreaks havoc on clarity and intuition. Take a short break whenever you feel yourself becoming stressed and find a quiet spot to practice deep breathing until you have released the stress from your body.

Get Creative!

Alternate the meditations and exercises regularly, and practice star gazing and moon gazing when the weather allows. Exercise or take nature walks at times when you can expose your body to orange sun rays. Incorporating superfoods for the health of the pineal gland and third eye chakra is as easy as stocking up and eating them as often as you can. Crystals, stones, and third eye chakra colors for your jewelry, wardrobe, and home require nothing more than the initial purchase—and shopping for them is loads of fun!

More importantly, don't beat yourself up if your schedule doesn't go like clockwork. Your third eye chakra won't immediately become dormant again if you miss a few exercises and meditation.

The great thing about the third eye chakra is that the more you begin to experience the benefits, the more motivated and excited you will become about doing meditation and exercises to develop this part of your life. They will never feel like a chore.

Get creative, be flexible, and enjoy your transformation. All of this will come together gradually as you explore and discover what suits you best.

Precautions

It would be dishonest not to mention certain precautions that you need to be aware of when awakening your third eye. You are embarking on a journey to a mysterious and unknown realm—and the journey is not without some dangers if you go in with your eyes closed.

1. Make sure you are emotionally prepared.

Awakening the third eye chakra is a very serious pursuit. Talking about all of the things you will experience when your third eye is opened sounds thrilling and exciting, and you are understandably eager to jump in and experience all of the benefits.

However, actually experiencing those results may scare and even terrify many people. You must be very aware of this fact: *Once the pineal gland and the inner eye chakra are opened, your consciousness will literally begin to expand, transcending the realm of the physical into a realm that you never imagined existed.* Take some time to let this sink in and make the intention to be emotionally strong.

In addition to the wonderful gifts you will receive, such as inner wisdom, inner peace, and greater intuition, you must be prepared for the possibility that you will see, hear, and feel things that may disturb or confuse you. It is good to be mentally prepared for these experiences, although they are rare.

2. Separating fact from fiction.

Some people claim that some of the things that you see in the spiritual realm could be demonic entities. This is absolutely false. Everything you experience in the non-physical realm is related solely to you. You may see different emotions and aspects of yourself that are being unleashed from your subconscious mind.

They have always existed, but now, your heightened consciousness is allowing you to see and experience them.

The inner eye is like a mirror that sometimes reflects your negative inner characteristics and emotions. They may sometimes take the form of scary visions or thoughts, but they are certainly not demonic—and can be resolved once they are revealed.

This is why opening the third eye chakra can be so transformative. It brings you in touch with aspects of your personality (usually not good ones) that have gone ignored. These aspects could be influencing your life, but you have refused to confront them. This is why you have buried them deep in your subconscious mind.

Just know that opening your third eye is not the run-of-the-mill self-help technique that will make you a better parent, a super-achiever, or a better lover. It is a serious business that comes with responsibility. You must feel completely ready and mentally prepared.

The Dangers of an Overactive Third Eye Chakra

An overactive third eye chakra, although not physically dangerous, may cause mental overwhelm and distress. Some of the manifestations include:

- Losing touch with reality and over-fantasizing.
- Becoming obsessed with psychic visions.
- Becoming irrationally afraid of psychic visions.
- Anxiety.
- Mental exhaustion, where you are bombarded with thoughts from the inner eye and become unable to focus clearly or make decisions.
- Feeling overwhelmed.
- Insomnia.
- Vision and sinus problems.

- Cloudy judgment.

- Difficulty distinguishing between reality and what you see in your third eye.

- Headaches.

- Hallucinations.

Balancing an Overactive Third Eye Chakra

These are common symptoms that occur when you do not properly ground yourself or when the chakra system is not aligned. The chakra spine meditation and regular mindfulness exercises should address both of these issues and restore the third eye chakra balance. In addition, you may do the following:

- If you feel overwhelmed by the intensity or frequency of psychic visions, meditate on your third eye; make the intention to slow them down; and ask your third eye to slow them down.

- Meditate on the root chakra in order to ground yourself firmly.

- If you are unable to articulate the thoughts coming from your third eye or feel they are affecting your clarity, slow them down by meditating on the sacral chakra.

- Meditation on the heart chakra will also bring more perspective and balance to your mental images and messages.

- Restore balance to your third eye chakra by eliminating sugar from your diet for a few days and eating loads of fresh vegetables, fruit, and whole-grain foods.

- Meditating with crystals on the third eye will also help, as their high vibration actually helps balance rather than overstimulate the third eye.

How to Balance an Overactive Pineal Gland

An overactive pineal gland can cause similar symptoms to that caused by the third eye chakra. This can be caused by a deficiency due to underexposure of light or excessive melatonin production due to overexposure to light. Needless to say, it can also throw your third eye chakra off balance as well. Here is what you can do to restore balance to your pineal gland:

- Go to bed at the same time each night and at a moderate hour.

- Sleep in a totally darkened room. Even light filtering in from a streetlight can be disruptive to an overactive pineal gland, so be aware of this.

- Use frankincense, sandalwood, and peppermint essential oils in a diffuser or put one or two drops directly on your third eye chakra. These oils are known for calming the pineal gland.

- Wear amber-tinted glasses starting in the late afternoon until night sets in.

- Practice third eye color visualization on the colors indigo and purple.

Dealing with Skepticism and Rejection

Although you should not go out of your way to advertise your gifts, they will eventually become noticed. If you are trying to help someone by reading their aura, again, you will have to explain a little bit about your special skills.

Reactions to your third eye powers will vary. Some people will be curious but open to learning more. Others will be fascinated and eager to hear all the details. People who are into spirituality, in particular, will feel immediate empathy and affinity with you.

Unfortunately, you may also face skepticism, ridicule, and be viewed as "One of those crackpots who think they're Harry Potter." Sometimes, you might encounter outright hostility. This usually comes from religious people who perceive such activities as demonic.

Some people may shun you, causing you to feel isolated and frustrated. Knowing how to deal with negative reactions is crucial for keeping you positive and preventing self-doubt. Here are some suggested steps:

• Speak to others calmly and in a matter of fact way about the gifts you are developing. You can give a brief history of the pineal gland and how it has long been believed to be the source of "inner knowing." Explain that you are simply developing that inner knowing and that you are living proof that it exists.

• Don't exaggerate your experiences or blow them out of proportion.

• Limit contact with people who are outright rude and hostile. Their negative energy will cause you to doubt yourself and limit the perception of your third eye.

• Although you may be brimming with inner wisdom and knowledge, don't expose it to others or talk about it. Simply show people your normal human side and let them see that your abilities do not make you less human or different.

• Excessive self-doubt can actually cause your third eye to close again. Believe in yourself and know that you are not alone. Surround yourself with positive, encouraging people who believe in you. This is why joining an online community is so important. Seek the support you need from like-minded people. You will discover that most of them have had similar experiences and that you are not alone.

Don't Expect Rapid Change

Unfortunately, there is no concrete—or even an estimated—timeframe in which you will begin to see changes. Some people may begin experiencing some sort of psychic gifts within weeks or months, while for others, it may take years. Some people will notice heightened perception and intuition fairly quickly but no psychic experience until much later. For the majority of people, the process is gradual and slow. Keeping this in mind will save you a lot of frustration!

Never rush the process or think that meditating ten times a day will open your third eye faster. Just maintain a consistent routine of meditation and other practices and trust—you must trust completely in your third eye.

More importantly, don't push it, and don't make yourself see things that aren't there. Many people tend to interpret all dreams and thoughts as messages from the third eye when they are not. Let your intuition guide you and not your wishful thinking!

Your third eye will never be 100% open. It is a skill that you will continue to develop throughout your lifetime. It is akin to the concept of Nirvana in Buddhism. A Buddhist strives to attain Nirvana and makes it his lifelong goal, knowing that he will never fully attain it. Yet, he willingly devotes his life to this noble journey because of the wisdom and spiritual enrichment it brings him.

That is the mindset that you need to adopt. Be grateful for every small step forward. Even small glimmers of insight can change your life forever. Stay open to receiving, don't expect too much too quickly, and know that change will happen.

Conclusion

The potential of the third eye chakra and the pineal gland is beyond imagination. Being able to harness even a tiny bit of that potential is really something that everyone should consider. We are all adventurous. We are all naturally curious. We long to discover new things, visit new places, and immerse ourselves in unique experiences. We tell ourselves that we are content with living normal lives and being like everyone else, but deep inside, every single one of us longs to be different.

All of our secret longings can be fulfilled by merely discovering and exploring the fathomless spiritual realm that exists with ourselves. It is through our inner eye that we can become unique and change our lives—because we will become our true higher selves and understand our purpose in life.

Let's conclude by exploring your own conclusions. How do you feel about everything you've learned from this book? Do you agree that opening your third eye chakra can transform your life?

As the first step in your spiritual journey of discovery, thank you for reading this book, *Third Eye Awakening: An Essential Guide to Opening Your Third Eye Chakra and Experiencing Higher Consciousness, Psychic Visions and Clairvoyance along with Tips for Balancing Chakras and Seeing Auras.*

If you choose to begin this lifelong inner journey to wisdom, knowledge, and indescribable inner peace and joy, congratulations, and best of luck!

Part 2: Psychic

A Psychic Development Guide for Tapping into Your Ability for Telepathy, Mediumship, Intuition, Aura Reading, Clairvoyance, Healing and Communicating with Your Spirit Guides

Introduction

Fascination with psychic abilities is something that has been on the rise in recent years. An ever-growing number of people are exploring topics that were relatively unheard of or considered taboo not that long ago. Things such as clairvoyance, telepathy, intuition, and even communicating with spirits are becoming more mainstream, with an increasing number of scientific experiments and case studies supporting the conclusion that these phenomena are demonstrably real. Even so, it is the fact that countless people are awakening to their psychic abilities that underlie the growing interest in such topics. More and more people are discovering certain inherent talents, ones that enable them to do things beyond what conventional wisdom would suggest is possible. The problem is that most of these people don't know the true nature of their abilities, nor how to harness and strengthen them, resulting in those talents largely going to waste.

Fortunately, the process of discovering and developing psychic abilities is far easier than most people realize. The truth of the matter is that everyone has psychic abilities of one form or another; they simply need to identify which ones they possess in order to begin fulfilling their full potential. This book will reveal how to determine what psychic abilities you possess, thereby enabling you to discover your inherent skills. It will also explore the numerous forms that psychic ability takes, showing you the differences and similarities between each of them. Finally, this book will delve into the methods and techniques for developing whatever psychic ability you possess. Everything from meditation techniques to instructions on how to communicate with spirits is covered, providing you with every tool necessary to begin your journey into the exciting and fulfilling world of psychic phenomena. By the time you finish reading this book, you will know exactly what talents you possess and how to develop those talents in order to transform your life into the happy and fulfilling one you both desire and deserve.

Chapter 1: The Psychic: What Does It Mean to Be Psychic?

The term "psychic" is one that almost everyone has heard at one point or another. One of the first images that may come to mind is that of an exotic woman promising to tell you what the future holds for only ten dollars a minute—a real bargain considering what's at stake. Another image might be of a person using their psychic abilities to tell what card a member of the audience is holding or to levitate a table in front of that same audience. Needless to say, most of these examples of psychic abilities are nothing more than parlor tricks, more often than not found in the same books that teach a person how to pull a rabbit out of a hat. Unfortunately, this false and hokey image of what a psychic is causes most people to dismiss the real phenomenon, one that affects virtually every single person daily. This results in countless people failing ever to tap into their true psychic potential and use their abilities to transform their lives. Therefore, it is important to properly define what it means to be psychic, thereby helping you to discover your abilities and talents.

What does the Term "Psychic" Really Mean?

Perhaps the best way to understand what the term "psychic" really means is to take a closer look at the word itself. The word comes from the Greek word "psyche", which means mind or soul. This is also the root word for such things as psychology, psychiatry, and psychosomatic. All of these words share a common meaning, namely the focus on the mind as opposed to the physical body. Anyone with a psychological condition is understood to have a problem emotionally or mentally, and thus in need of treatment that focuses on the heart and mind. The very same thing holds true for someone with psychic abilities. In this case, rather than having a negative condition, such a person will have special skills relating to their emotional and mental perception of the world around them. In short, someone with psychic abilities can gain information or perform a task without using their five physical senses.

Numerous ancient traditions embrace the notion that the soul of a person has the same sensory capabilities as that of their body. In other words, just as the body can see and hear, so too, the soul of an individual can also see and hear, albeit without having to rely on physical hearing or sight. Not only does this enable a person to see beyond their physical space or hear beyond the range of physical hearing, but it also enables them to see things that would otherwise be invisible and hear things that would otherwise be silent. Thoughts, for example, cannot be heard with the physical ear since they make no physical sound. However, they can be heard with the "mind's ear" since they exist in the realm of the mind. The ability to hear things with the mind is known as clairaudience, which means "clear hearing".

The same phenomenon can be found in terms of seeing. Clairvoyance, or "clear seeing", is the ability to see with the mind. This allows a person to see beyond what their physical eyes can perceive. Such things as future events, far away events, or even the intentions of another person can be seen with the mind's eye. Another term that is used to describe such abilities is "supernatural", which in its purest definition means "above natural". Unfortunately, this term has also come to mean many different things, resulting in more confusion than clarification when used. However, in its truest form, supernatural simply implies that an event or ability is beyond what the five physical or natural senses can achieve. This is perhaps the best and most concise definition of psychic phenomena and abilities that can be found.

One of the most common mistakes many people make is to assume that all psychic abilities are essentially the same. A good example of this can be seen in the area of mediumship. A medium is someone who can convey messages and visions to a person by tapping into the spirit realm. More often than not, such individuals are labeled as fortune tellers, and thus dismissed as tricksters and fakes. Another term often used to categorize such individuals is that of psychic. Herein lies a very important distinction. While all mediums are psychics, not all psychics are mediums. It's a bit like saying that while all Californians are Americans, not all Americans are Californians. Not only do the vast majority of Americans not live in California, but most have never even visited the state. The very same thing holds true for psychics. A person can have psychic abilities but not be able to read a person's mind or see far off events. The fact of the matter is that there are numerous different categories of psychic abilities, each with even their own unique skills and qualities, making it so that almost no two psychics are exactly the same.

Who has Psychic Potential?

This distinction is vital when it comes to being able to determine your unique psychic abilities. Just because you don't have vivid dreams, or you can't sense what another person is thinking is no reason to believe that you have no abilities whatsoever. Again, there are numerous different types of psychic abilities, and thus it is important to keep an open mind when trying to discover your personal potential. The bottom line is that everyone has psychic potential of one form or another. This is because everyone is, in essence, a spirit being, or a soul. Therefore, just as anyone with a physical body will have physical senses, so too, anyone with a spirit or a soul will have psychic abilities. The trick is to discover what abilities you possess in abundance.

Once again, this is another example of how psychic senses and physical senses are a direct reflection of one another. Although everyone has a physical body, that doesn't mean that everyone has the same eyesight or the same ability to hear sound. While some people have very keen eyesight, allowing them to read extra fine print or to see something far away with great clarity and detail, others require reading glasses to see that fine print, or prescription glasses to see far off distances. Others still may not be able to see at all, forcing them to rely on their other physical senses in order to perceive the world around them. A blind person may use their sense of touch to help them read, as in the case of Braille, or to visualize what a person looks like. This is precisely how psychic abilities work as well. Just because everyone has a soul, it doesn't mean that everyone can read minds or predict the future. While some may possess such skills in high degrees, others will find themselves virtually blind and deaf in such areas.

Needless to say, the important thing isn't necessarily to fix the wrong things. Rather than trying to develop skill sets that you lack or that you struggle with, the trick is to discover your strengths and develop them to the highest level possible. A good way to envision this is to imagine a baseball team. A good coach allows the pitcher to hone their pitching skills while allowing their best hitters to hone their batting skills. You wouldn't see a pitcher being made to improve their batting, nor a hitter forced to develop pitching skills. The name of the game is to play everyone to their strengths. That holds true for psychic abilities. If you can't see auras, then don't waste your time trying to develop the skill. Instead, find the skill you currently have, the one that is inherent to your abilities. Once you find that, the next step is to nurture it and develop it so that it can serve you in your day-to-day life, thereby taking your life to a whole new level.

That said, some people are indeed more gifted than others when it comes to psychic abilities. Fortunately, there are a few simple tests that can help to identify whether a person is gifted with strong psychic abilities or not. One such test is in the area of dreams. If you have a rich dream life, wherein you experience vivid and engaging dreams regularly, the chances are that you have strong psychic abilities. In fact, the ability to recall dreams is another indicator of psychic potential. If you often have gut feelings, such as to avoid certain people or situations, then you are probably a natural psychic. Visions of future events, the ability to feel another person's emotions, or read their thoughts are also signs of heightened psychic ability. The reason that such events indicate psychic potential is that they all rely on no physical senses. Thus, a person who can dream vividly and recall their dreams uses their mind's eye in a very real way. Someone who has gut feelings is in touch with their intuition, and so on. You are probably reading this book because you have discovered a pattern in your life, one in which your psychic ability has shown itself and is now waiting for you to respond and give it the attention it deserves.

How can Psychic Abilities Impact your Day-to-Day Life?

Like any abilities, psychic abilities can be used in a vast number of ways to improve and even transform a person's day-to-day life. One example of this is in the area of intuition. Many people have to make decisions daily that will impact their lives in one way or another. They might have to buy a car, look for a job, or even hire a person to work for them. Although a good deal of factual information is usually available to help in making such decisions, there can also be a fair amount of guesswork involved. This is where intuition can make all the difference. Rather than having to guess whether or not you will be happy in a given job, or whether a candidate is truly as good as their résumé makes them appear to be, you can use intuition to see beyond the facts and determine the truth of a situation. This can help you to make the best choice every time, avoiding mistakes and regrets that can undermine your happiness or even your very chance of success.

Dreams can also come in handy when making all-important decisions. Many people have heard someone say, "Let me sleep on it," at one time or another. Although this statement usually indicates a person's desire to give a decision some extra thought, the truth is that someone with psychic abilities could literally "sleep on it", allowing their dreams to reveal the outcome of one decision or another. Such practices have been recorded throughout human history in virtually every corner of the globe. Using dreams to make decisions or understand the nature of complex events can help you to cheat by literally skipping ahead to see what awaits down each path at your disposal. This can not only take away the guesswork to a decision, but it can also ensure that you make the best decision every single time. Furthermore, numerous case studies have revealed how inventors, artists, and musicians have used their dreams to solve problems or unlock their true potential. Not only *can* such an ability be the difference between success and failure, but it has been proven.

Intuition can also help you to engage more meaningfully with those around you, thereby improving your relationships in a very real and significant way. A good example of this is in the area of empathy. An empath is someone who can tap into the emotions of another person, virtually feeling what they feel. One way this can help is to protect you from those who would cheat or deceive you, such as corrupt business people, false friends, or anyone who would seek to take advantage of you. By feeling another person's emotional state, you can determine their sincerity or lack thereof. However, the main application for empathy is the ability to know how a person feels so that you can better connect with them and help them through their time of struggle. By sharing another person's pain, you can prove more capable when it comes to saying the right thing or even giving the best advice. This ability will help you to feel connected to everyone around you in a way that will transform how you experience life itself. No longer will you feel as though you are an individual, making your way alone through life. Instead, you will understand that all living beings are connected, and this will make you realize that no one is ever truly alone.

Establishing Rules to Ensure Better Control of your Abilities

Of course, it goes without saying that strong abilities bring strong responsibilities. Nowhere is this notion truer than in the area of psychic abilities. Subsequently, it is absolutely vital that in addition to discovering and honing your abilities, you also establish a set of rules that will serve to protect you as well as those around you. Without such rules, you will inevitably find yourself in a situation in which others can cause you harm or in which you bring harm to others. Since psychic abilities come from the soul, such harm would be felt on the soul level, making it that much harder to recover from. Therefore, preventing such incidents is critical as it will enable you to avoid considerable hardship and regret all around.

One of the most important rules is that of giving yourself the time and space you need to recharge your batteries. More often than not, people who discover and develop their psychic abilities do so intending to help others around them. The ability to connect to the feelings of others, heal the pains and ills of others, or even tap into the spirit realm to foretell another person's destiny are all noble pursuits, but they all come at a cost. Every psychic activity takes energy to perform, much like every purchase you make requires cash. As such, if you aren't careful, you can use up all of your energy trying to save the world, just like you can spend all of your money if you go on a shopping spree. Therefore, the trick is to budget yourself when it comes to the time and energy you spend helping others. One of the best rules is to give yourself plenty of downtime daily or fairly regularly, thereby enabling you to recharge your batteries and restore tranquility to your mind. This will keep you from becoming burned out, or even worse, depressed and overwhelmed.

Another critical rule to employ is that of respecting other people's privacy. Just because you can read another person's thoughts doesn't mean you should. Nor does it mean that they want you to. A good rule of thumb that will help you to respect others is only to use your abilities when it is necessary for your personal wellbeing. Thus, tapping into the heart or mind of someone trying to sell you a car or applying for a job is perfectly reasonable. Reading the mind of the person sitting next to you on the bus for kicks, on the other hand, is less than decent. Therefore, only ever use your abilities in a way that is necessary and beneficial to all involved. Never abuse your skills, and never use them to intimidate others.

Some Examples of Real Psychic Events

While almost everyone contemplates psychic abilities at one time or another, most dismiss their existence altogether, citing a lack of evidence to support their existence. Fortunately, there are a growing number of case studies and personal accounts that will offer the evidence needed to inspire people to take psychic phenomena more seriously. The following are just a few examples of real-life psychic events, some that changed lives on a personal level, while others changed the world as we know it.

One story involves a journalist who was interviewing a medium for a story. After the interview, the medium offered a free reading for the journalist. Although skeptical, she agreed, not knowing what to expect. Immediately the medium told her of a woman that he saw, one whose description and name matched that of her long-dead grandmother. Next, he told her of a man with the woman, and the description matched that of her more recently departed father. The man had a message for his wife, the medium said. That message was that it was time to get rid of his neckties. After the reading, the journalist called her mother and asked if she had gotten rid of her father's clothes yet, something she had hesitated to do. The mother said she had gotten rid of everything *except* his neckties.

Another story involves a man who had gone AWOL from the army while serving in Vietnam. While on shore leave back in the States, he decided to not return to duty. During that time, he visited a friend who was skilled at divination. He conducted an I Ching reading, which revealed that a long trip over a great body of water would prove beneficial. The friend decided to go back to Vietnam, despite wanting to leave the army. Upon his return, the number of troops in Vietnam was reduced, and he was given a regular discharge, allowing him to leave the army and return home legally.

Dreams have served to shape decisions and discoveries, many of which have changed the world in ways most people don't realize. Elias Howe, for example, struggled with designing the mechanical sewing machine. After several failed attempts, he was almost bankrupt when one night, he dreamt of where the needle needed to go in order for the machine to work properly. Upon waking, he drew the design, a design that became patented and is still used in modern sewing machine models today.

Niels Bohr, a pioneer in modern physics, had a dream in which he saw the planets orbiting the sun. He realized that this dream was the answer to his search for the model of an atom. Using his dream imagery, he was able to prove the structure of the atom, which is responsible for shaping such things as atomic energy. Albert Einstein dreamt of an experience in which he was sledding downhill on a snowy mountain. He began going so fast that he almost reached the speed of light. At that moment, the appearance of the stars changed, leading him to discover the Theory of Relativity.

Countless more examples of dreams, readings, visions, and the like that have changed lives can be found all around the world. However, such stories are in the end just that—stories. The important thing is to find your own proof, your own evidence. Fortunately, everyone has had experiences that they can't explain in simple, natural terms. Those experiences are the fingerprints of psychic activity, usually involving their personal psychic abilities. Rather than looking to other accounts as proof, you should look to them for direction, helping you to recall and recognize the evidence you have within your life, the evidence of your psychic potential.

Chapter 2: Meditation: The First Step

One of the principal tools for developing psychic abilities is the practice of meditation. This practice has been around for thousands of years, helping countless people around the world to achieve numerous benefits and breakthroughs. In fact, tradition states that the Buddha himself achieved enlightenment as a result of his meditative practices. Fortunately, you don't need to be searching for truth or enlightenment to make use of this valuable tool. Millions of people around the world today use enlightenment for various reasons, including everything from spiritual development to stress relief and physical restoration. This chapter will provide a basic understanding of what meditation is, as well as the various ways in which it can help you to nurture and hone your psychic skills. Furthermore, there will be instructions on a few forms of meditation to help you get started with a practice that will provide you with a solid foundation for your quest to become a proficient psychic.

A Basic Overview of Meditation

When most people think of meditation, they envision Buddhist monks dressed in their robes, chanting as they allow their minds to transcend physical reality and touch the realm of spirit. While this is one aspect of meditation, it is not the be-all and end-all of the practice. A good way to understand meditation is to think of it as a gym of sorts. When you go to a gym, you can choose to do any number of exercise routines, ranging from free weights, aerobic exercises, general strength training, or even just getting on an exercise bike or a treadmill to shake up an otherwise sedentary life. Each type of routine offers specific benefits and results, meaning that no two people will necessarily have the same experience. This is precisely how meditation works.

Overall, the fundamentals of meditation are generally the same from one form to another, despite the numerous and distinct differences that make each form very unique. The basic premise is that the practitioner finds a quiet location where they can be alone and uninterrupted for a specified period. Within that period, they will begin to shut out external influences and distractions, focusing on their internal reality instead. More often than not, breathing plays a central role in the practice, providing the individual with a focus point that enables them to achieve the calm and mindful state they are aiming for. Sitting in a comfortable yet upright position is also central to just about all forms of meditation. Beyond that, however, the other elements tend to be specific to the various versions, thereby creating a different experience that allows a person to achieve different results.

Mindfulness, for example, is a common goal shared by most practitioners of meditation. Certain forms of meditation allow you to develop your sense of mental focus and clarity, removing the clutter that fills most people's minds daily. Relaxation is another benefit that comes from most forms of meditation, including that known as body scan meditation. This form is also used to send healing and restorative energy to parts of the body that are suffering in one way or another. In short, there are two main categories of meditation: calming and insightful. Calming meditation is those techniques that focus on stress relief of both the body and mind. Alternatively, insightful meditation techniques are those that focus on sharpening mental and physical awareness.

There is one more distinction worth mentioning in terms of the different forms of meditative practice, namely that of guided and unguided meditation. Guided meditation simply suggests that you practice under the instruction of a guide. That guide can be an actual person, such as a spiritual instructor, or it can be a pre-recorded message that takes you through the steps and helps you to understand the process every step of the way. Unguided meditation simply indicates that you perform your practice alone and in silence—at least in the case of those techniques that are practiced in solitude. It is often recommended that beginners engage in guided meditation first in order to better understand the practice. This also gives them the chance to ask questions or raise concerns in the event they meditate in the presence of an actual guide.

How Meditation Helps Develop Psychic Abilities

The question many people ask is how meditation can help develop psychic abilities. Truth be told, there are several ways in which meditative practices can help anyone to discover, nurture, and hone their psychic skills. One of the most immediate ways that meditation achieves this goal is that it helps the individual to clear their heart and mind of all the clutter and chaos that ordinarily affects them. This condition is commonly referred to as "monkey mind" in the Buddhist tradition. Simply put, most people have any number of thoughts, concerns, images, and even songs running through their minds at any given time. This noise only serves to make it harder to connect with intuition, insight, and other psychic abilities that require a mind that is calm and focused in order to be heard. By removing the noise, meditation can create the environment necessary for effective psychic activity.

Another way in which meditation helps to improve psychic abilities is to increase mental clarity and awareness. Techniques for achieving this goal fall under the insightful category. A person who practices insightful meditation will exercise their mind and awareness in a way that hones their ability to resist distractions and become aware of the energies within and around them. As mentioned earlier, all psychic activity involves the mind in one way or another. Therefore, any exercise that strengthens the mind and improves such things as focus, perception, and mental discipline will naturally strengthen a person's psychic abilities. In a way, it's a bit like when sports players go to the gym to work out. To the average person, it might seem strange that lifting weights could help someone play soccer better. However, to the athlete, it makes perfect sense since the stronger their body is, the better their performance on the pitch. Meditation is exactly like that. It strengthens the muscles needed to perform psychic activities to the best of a person's abilities.

The third and least known way that meditation helps to develop psychic abilities is that it helps a person connect with their inner voice. Whether the goal is to shut out external distractions or to eliminate internal noise, the outcome of meditation is largely the same, namely an increased sense of intuition. After all, once all the distraction is gone, the only thing left is the true voice of the individual. This voice is that which is referred to as intuition, or a person's gut feeling. The stronger this voice becomes, the stronger a person's psychic abilities become. Additionally, meditation can help an individual to connect to their spirit guides. Just as hearing the inner voice is essential for psychic practice, so too, hearing the voice of spirit guides is equally critical. Therefore, meditation is a crucial tool as it helps a person to discover and connect to that part of them that is the very heart of any psychic ability. Added to the increase of mindfulness and the decrease of distraction, it's no wonder that the most effective psychics are those who practice meditation regularly, if not daily.

How to Perform Mindfulness Meditation

Mindfulness meditation allows a person to develop their ability to be fully present in the moment. This is vital for anyone who wants to tap into their intuition for guidance or answers. Furthermore, it is a good way to help a person tune in to their spirit guides. The steps for performing mindfulness meditation are as follows:

- The first step for just about every meditation practice is to find a quiet place where you can be alone and uninterrupted for a specified period. This will help you to focus on your practice as you won't be distracted or even listening for potential distractions to occur.
- When you have your location picked out, the next thing you need to do is to sit comfortably. Sitting cross-legged on a cushion or mat on the floor is ideal, but not necessary. A chair will also suffice provided it allows you to sit upright, keeping a good posture that allows for good, deep breathing. The important thing is to keep your spine straight, thus allowing your breath and energy to flow evenly throughout your body. Your upper arms should hang loosely by your side while your hands can be allowed to rest in your lap in whatever way feels most comfortable.
- Next, you need to start focusing on your breathing. Begin to take deeper breaths, ones that are relaxing and restorative. Although your goal is to breathe deeper, your breathing should still be natural and unforced, thereby increasing relaxation to your body and mind.
- Once your breathing is regulated, the next step is to become aware of your surroundings. Take a moment to recognize the sights, sounds, and even smells of your environment. However, don't allow your thoughts to dwell on one thing for too long. The goal is to become aware, nothing more, nothing less. Therefore, observe one thing or event for about ten seconds, then move on to another.
- Your mind will begin to fixate on things from time to time, evoking memories or judgments depending on the item or event you are observing. Whenever this happens, simply let go of the thought process and return to simply observing your surroundings. The most important thing is to be wholly present in body and mind.

- Finally, recognize that your mind is simply doing its job by dredging up thoughts, concerns, and memories based on what you are observing. This isn't a bad thing as such, merely a habit that you are beginning to break. Don't be too harsh on yourself whenever this happens. Simply allow your distracting thoughts to evaporate and return your focus to your present moment. The more you practice this form of meditation, the less distracted your mind will become.
- Once you have perfected the skill of directing your mind from distraction to the here and now you can begin to practice mindfulness meditation in a more public setting. The same principles apply, except now you can shift your attention from one person to another or from one event to another, allowing yourself to observe without judging or becoming fixated on any one thing or person. Needless to say, never perform this kind of exercise while driving a car or operating machinery that requires your full attention.

How to Perform Visualization Meditation

Visualization meditation is a practice that helps an individual hone their ability to connect to objects and people remotely. This means you can see a person or a thing without having to be anywhere near them. Needless to say, such a vision involves the mind's eye rather than the physical eye. The steps for performing visualization meditation are as follows:

- Find a quiet place where you will be alone and uninterrupted for the time you need for your meditative practice. It is important to establish how long you want to spend so that you ensure yourself the best chance for success.
- Sit in a cross-legged position with your spine straight, your upper arms relaxed by your sides, and your hands resting comfortably in your lap. This posture will help to relax your body and improve your breathing and blood flow, thus increasing your mental awareness.

- Once you have achieved a comfortable position, you can begin to establish your deep, relaxed breathing routine. Start taking longer, deeper breaths, ones that relax you while providing the oxygen needed to restore your physical and mental energies.
- The next step is for beginners. This step has you observe an object in front of you. It can be any object at all, and you can pick and choose an object to meditate on to make it easier. Simply stare at the object for a minute or so, taking in every detail you can.
- Next, close your eyes and begin to visualize the object you observed. Allow your mind to recall all of the details you can remember, using your imagination to recreate the object in as much detail as possible. You can even imagine yourself moving around the object, seeing it from all sides. However, you should remain seated, only moving in your mind.
- Once you have clearly visualized your chosen object, you can begin to visualize something else. This can be another object, such as something else in the room, or even something elsewhere, such as your car or your neighbor's mailbox. Alternatively, you can choose to visualize a person, picturing them where you imagine them to be. No matter what you choose to visualize, the trick is to visualize your subject with as much detail as possible, even allowing yourself to observe the surroundings.
- Next, start to take note of the specific details you notice. For example, if you visualize your neighbor's mailbox, is the flag up or down? Is the sky clear or cloudy? What specific features can you pick out? In the case of a person, where are they? Are they at home or work? Are they talking to a person, working on the computer, or making a phone call? How do they appear emotionally? All of these details can prove important in terms of psychic ability. While your mind might begin by using memory to create the vision of a person or object, eventually, it will connect to the subject in real-

time, allowing you to observe things in your mind's eye that your physical senses would be unable to detect.

- Finally, take note of any specific details that stand out. If you envision a person and you see them having a bad day, call them later and ask them how their day was. Again, initial results may be irregular, but over time, you will discover that your observations will become more and more accurate, enabling you to connect to any object or person without having to leave the comfort of your home.

How to Perform Psychic Meditation

Psychic meditation is the form of meditation that really allows a person to tap into their psychic skills. Specifically, it hones a person's ability to see, feel, and hear information on the spirit level. Images, whispers, sensations, and the like all become more regular and more pronounced the more a person practices psychic meditation. The steps for performing psychic meditation are as follows:

- As with any form of meditation, the first step is always to find a quiet place that offers privacy as well as solitude. Unplug any phones and remove any other forms of distraction, ensuring the most peaceful environment possible.
- Next, sit on the floor, using a mat or a cushion for comfort, in a cross-legged position. Although you want to be relaxed, it is vital to ensure that your spine is straight, as this will increase blood and oxygen flow throughout the body. Again, your upper arms should hang freely by your sides, and your hands should be relaxed in your lap.
- Once you have your location and posture sorted, the next step is to focus on your breathing, ensuring your breaths are deep but relaxed, not forced or strained. As you focus on your breathing, allow your body to relax and clear your mind of any extra thoughts or distractions.

- Next, close your eyes and begin to observe any images, feelings, sounds, or impulses that occur out of the blue. At first, you might find your mind still full of thoughts and images from your day's activities. If this is the case, take more time to focus on your breathing and thus clear your mind of clutter and noise. However, once your mind is clear, any images, sounds, and the like should be observed and contemplated.
- Take the time to consider every impulse you get, whether it's a physical sensation, an emotional reaction, or an image, word, or some other form of information, no matter how random it may seem. In fact, the more random it is, the more likely it is to be psychic in nature rather than the product of your imagination. If you feel an emotion, take the time to consider what the emotion is and what might be causing it. Is it a warning? Is it for someone else? Or is someone thinking about you? If you see an image of a friend or a loved one, contemplate that image carefully. Are they happy, or are they in need of your love and support? The important thing is to open your mind to all input from the spirit realm. Again, at first, you might struggle to differentiate between figments of your imagination and the voice of your spirit guides. However, with practice, the ability to know the difference will strengthen, allowing you to hear the voice of the Universe as clearly as you hear a voice on the other end of a phone.
- Once you have ended your meditation, you must take the time to reconnect to your immediate surroundings. This will close your mind to the constant flow of information that would otherwise overwhelm you as you go about your regular day. The best way to achieve this goal is to practice a short round of mindfulness meditation, thereby reconnecting to your environment and restoring your mind to its normal function.

- The two most important things to remember concerning psychic meditation are to be open-minded and patient. Only by being open-minded can you receive the information you are seeking. And only by being patient can you develop your skills to the level you desire. Nothing worth doing is ever easy, so don't be frustrated if results are slow and erratic. With a little effort and patience, you will begin to achieve the results you desire, and then your psychic abilities will rise to levels you never imagined possible.

Improving Meditation with Yoga

One way to take your meditation practice to the next level is to incorporate it with the practice of yoga. This helps align your body and mind in a way that creates a certain singularity of being. The more singular you are as a person is the clearer and more present you are at any given time. Therefore, it is recommended that once you have gained familiarity and even success with meditation, you should begin to add yoga to your routine to increase your abilities even further.

The basic principle of yoga is to stretch the body to improve blood flow and oxygen flow to all parts of the body, including the brain. This will have profound effects on your physical health and wellbeing as well as your mental health and wellbeing. Fortunately, there are many different forms of yoga, each designed for specific needs. Some are relatively easy, making it ideal for beginners or anyone with physical restrictions. Additionally, low-level yoga can be practiced alone, at home, and in very short amounts of time. Intermediate and high-level yoga should initially be practiced under the supervision of a certified instructor. You can start practicing alone once you are more experienced. Countless online resources will help you to get started with practicing yoga, thus enabling you to get a feel for it in order to see what forms are right for you. Additionally, the widespread practice of yoga means that there are groups virtually everywhere, allowing you to get the supervision you need as a beginner or as someone who likes to share their experience with others.

Chapter 3: Intuition

If you ask the average person on the street whether or not they have ever had a "gut feeling" about a person, place, or situation that proved to be true, almost everyone will tell you they have. This phenomenon is so common that few people ever pay any attention to it. Unfortunately, this means that only a handful of individuals take the time to discover the true nature of that gut feeling, including where it comes from, how it could be so accurate, and how to hone it for future use. In the end, this enigmatic gut feeling is but one example of intuition.

The simple fact of the matter is that intuition is the very language of the soul. It is how the soul communicates to the conscious and intellectual mind of an individual. As mentioned earlier, every person has both physical and non-physical senses, all of which send information to a person regarding their life, environment, and the choices at hand. Just as thoughts transmit physical information to the mind, intuition transmits non-physical information to the mind, providing insights far beyond what the physical senses can perceive. Understanding this language is the very foundation for developing any psychic ability. This chapter will explore the phenomenon of intuition, including its nature, the various forms it takes, methods for discovering and strengthening intuition, and some real-life examples of intuition at work. By the time you finish reading this chapter, you will have all the tools you need to begin tapping into your intuition, thereby discovering your full psychic potential.

What Exactly is Intuition?

Depending on whom you ask, intuition can mean any number of things. Some see it as a source of inherent knowledge, the ability to know something without having any logical or rational information to base that knowledge on. Others will define intuition as an inspiration of sorts, allowing a person to recognize opportunities as they arise or find solutions to problems that the intellect simply cannot provide. In the end, although these answers may seem vastly different, they are all correct. Intuition is the language that the soul uses to convey information to the mind. Therefore, whether the soul is telling the individual of upcoming opportunities, danger lurking around the corner, or some other necessary piece of information, intuition is the language it will use to convey the message.

Because intuition has many different faces, it has come to be called by many different names over time. In today's world, one of the most common names given to intuition is "gut feeling" or "gut instinct". Although the term "instinct" can mean something quite different from intuition, the way it is used to describe a feeling that acts as a warning, identifies it with intuition in this case. However, intuition has been known by other names throughout history and in the countless cultures that have spanned the globe. In Ancient Greece, a person's intuition was often seen as the voice of the gods themselves, offering divine inspiration or advice. Artists would attribute their intuitive abilities to the muses, while seers would give the Fates credit for the visions they had. It can be argued that the "voice of God" is another name for intuition, something that permeates Christian traditions all around the world today. In the end, no matter what culture or time you observe, you will find a widely recognized and respected phenomenon that clearly reflects intuition.

The real question is, "How does intuition affect psychic abilities?" To best understand this, you need to appreciate the value of language. If you were to move to another country, one that didn't speak English, the only way you would be able to get around in that country effectively would be to learn the language the natives spoke. Until you learn their language, everything they say to you will sound like gibberish, while everything you say to them will seem equally strange to their ears. This is where learning a language can make all the difference. Once you study their words, you can begin to understand what they say, while also developing the ability to speak directly to them. Anyone who has ever lived abroad will know just how big the difference can be once you can communicate in the native tongue.

This same relationship exists between the conscious mind and the soul. No matter how hard a person tries, they will never be able to teach their soul to speak in logical, rational terms. Therefore, to communicate clearly with the soul, to understand what the soul has to say, it is vital to learn the language of intuition. Only then can you take the otherwise gibberish sounds, images, and feelings and translate them into the meaningful messages that they are. When you master the language of intuition, you can communicate with your soul and spirit guides in real-time, allowing you to receive and transmit valuable information across time and space, giving you untold advantages when it comes to living your day-to-day life. Fortunately, learning the language of intuition is far easier than learning an actual language with grammar, syntax, and many words and phrases to memorize. However, make no mistake; the language of intuition can prove to be the richest, most complex language you will ever come upon.

Who has Intuition?

If the biggest question about intuition is what its nature truly is, the second biggest question must necessarily be, "Who has intuition?" The answer is both simple and complex. In short, everyone has intuition. Every single living being has the language of the soul, since, in theory, every single living being has a soul. This means that every person has intuition at their disposal, whether they realize it or not. Furthermore, numerous studies have indicated that animals and even plants have measurable levels of intuition. Needless to say, this is a huge concept to wrap your mind around. However, if you recognize that the soul is the essence of life, then all living things must have a soul of sorts, and thus intuition to some degree.

What makes the answer to the question "Who has intuition?" complex is that intuition is not a static quantity. In other words, it's not like asking, "Who has a head?" or "Who can breathe air?" Both of those answers are fixed. Everyone has a head, and everyone can breathe, and for the most part, both of those things are largely equal from one person to the next. However, when it comes to intuition, the value is fluid in nature. A good way to understand this is to consider the question, "Who has muscles?" Well, everyone has muscles since muscles are an integral part of the human body. However, it is not true that everyone's muscles are equal or that everyone has the same potential for muscle development. The wimpy 100-pound kid walking past the gym does not have the same muscular build of the 250-pound bodybuilder in the gym. They both have the same muscles, but to different degrees and with different levels of potential. Even if the wimpy kid went into the gym and worked out, he may never reach the same levels as a bodybuilder with natural ability. This is precisely how intuition works.

In short, everyone is born with intuition, just like everyone is born with muscles. Some have a certain natural potential, giving them stronger intuition without even having to try, whereas others may have to struggle, or at the very least, work harder in order to develop their intuitive capabilities. Furthermore, those who put in the time and effort daily to develop and strengthen their intuition will become far stronger over time than those who don't. Therefore, while everyone has intuition, it doesn't mean that everyone can simply tell you what card you are holding, or tap into your long-departed relative's mind to convey a message they want you to hear. Such gifts are unique to specific individuals, and even then, they must be honed and nurtured to achieve their fullest effect. The trick is to discover your inherent potential concerning intuition, and then take the time to develop that potential to its fullest.

Different Forms of Intuition

As already discussed, not all intuitions are alike. Subsequently, there are many different "languages" spoken by the soul, each unique to the individual. Some people will be gifted with the ability to see things with their mind's eye, whereas others will be more gifted when it comes to "feeling their way" through a situation, making the right decisions without any forehand knowledge or experience. Fortunately, these various forms of intuition can be sorted into a few categories, making it easier to understand and manage. Although there are as many as six or seven different categories, depending on the tradition you explore, this section will deal with the four most common. These four forms are known as clairvoyance, clairaudience, clairsentience, and claircognizance.

Clairvoyance is the ability to see clearly with the mind's eye. Some people may consider this to be a form of imagination, and in truth, a person's imagination can have a great impact on their clairvoyant capabilities. However, the basic element of clairvoyance is the ability to see within the mind a person, place, or event as clearly as if you were observing those things with your physical eye. People with this ability can see future events, far off events, or even the faces of people whom they will see unexpectedly in the day to come. Simply put, clairvoyance is the visual language of the soul. It is when the soul sends a picture to the individual in an attempt to inform them of something significant. Most people dismiss such images as clutter in their minds, only to recall them later on, after the event or person in the image has presented themselves in real life. In contrast, those who recognize and develop this skill can use those images to be better prepared for the events about to unfold in their life, thus enabling them to take full advantage of those events when they happen.

Clairaudience is the language of intuition based on sound. Often referred to as a person's "inner voice", this is when the soul sends information to the person's mind in the form of spoken words. Needless to say, this isn't the same phenomenon as experienced by people having schizophrenic episodes where voices in their heads are telling them to commit atrocities; however, the voice of the soul can sound just as real to a person as the voice of their conscious mind. In fact, when a person develops their clairaudience to high levels, they can virtually have an internal dialogue between their conscious and subconscious mind, discussing and debating the issue at hand. The inner voice is perhaps the second most common form of intuition experienced by countless people all around the world. While some recognize it as intuition, others attribute it to God, guardian angels, spirit guides, and the like. The truth is that all of these things may be correct. Clairaudience simply indicates that a person receives intuitive thought through the spoken word. Where those words are spoken from is another conversation altogether.

If clairaudience is the second most popular form of intuition, *clairsentience* is probably the most common. This is when intuition takes the shape of a feeling, specifically a gut feeling. The term "I have a bad feeling about this" is all but cliché—having been used so many times and in many different settings. Even so, the reason it has been used so often comes down to that just about everyone can relate to it. Therefore, almost everyone has had an experience of clairsentience in their lifetime. More often than not, it comes when an individual has a good or bad feeling about someone else, giving them a direction when it comes to making decisions regarding that other person. In the case of having a bad feeling about someone, an individual can take better precautions in order to safeguard their wellbeing. Alternatively, in the event a person gets a good feeling about someone, it may indicate the potential for a thriving friendship, or in many cases, even marriage. What makes clairsentience significant is its almost perfect accuracy, demonstrating the very real nature of intuition and the information it has to offer.

Finally, there is *claircognizance*. This is perhaps the rarest of all forms of intuition, taking the shape of a person having an inherent knowledge of something they have no experience or training in. To the casual observer, it can appear as though a situation or an object simply reveals itself to a person with claircognizance, as if they were seeing an instruction manual no one else could see. Such a person may walk to where they need to be in a strange place without needing directions or a map. Alternatively, they may pick up a complex instrument and simply know how to use it, as though they had been using it their whole life. Individuals with this form of intuition are usually quick learners as they combine their cognitive skills with their intuition, allowing them to learn something both consciously and subconsciously at the same time. If you have ever just "known" a thing, an answer to a question, or how to perform a new task, you have probably tapped into your claircognizant potential without realizing it.

Some Examples of Real-Life Intuition

There are many examples of real-life intuition stories in which a person used their inherent knowledge to make a decision that later turned out to be highly important, even to the point of saving people's lives. One such example occurred when an airplane was sitting on the runway waiting to take off. A passenger heard a strange noise and became highly alarmed. At first, she addressed it with the other passengers around her, all of whom dismissed her concerns as nonsense. She eventually got the attention of the crew, who also assured her there was no need for concern. Undeterred, she refused to settle down until the plane was inspected. Upon inspection, a serious defect was discovered, one that would almost certainly have resulted in the plane crashing while in flight, potentially killing all on board. This example could fall under several categories of intuition, including clairaudience for hearing the sound, and clairsentience for having a bad feeling that simply would not go away.

Certain cultures treat intuition with far greater respect and acceptance, resulting in a seamless integration of intuition into day-to-day life. Perhaps the best example of this is Ayurvedic Medicine. This is the traditional form of medicine that has been practiced in India for nearly five thousand years. It involves the doctor taking the patient's pulse using three fingers, enabling them to determine energy imbalances within the individual, as well as potential ways of treating them. This clearly mixes intellect with intuition, providing a more holistic approach to both illness and the methods for treating it. Needless to say, doctors in this tradition need to be as highly skilled in the psychic arts as they are in the science of medicine.

Unfortunately, most people have experienced intuition in the sense that they ignore the message they hear, only to discover its significance when it's too late. One example of this is when a woman needed to reach something on a high shelf in her home. As she grabbed a nearby chair to stand on, she heard a voice telling her not to use that chair, virtually shouting the warning to her. Dismissing the warning, she proceeded to stand on the chair, which immediately shattered under her, leaving her on the floor in pain with a dislocated elbow. While in the hospital, she vowed to always listen to that voice in the future as it had proven its value beyond any reasonable doubt.

How to Develop your Intuitive Abilities

Again, although everyone has intuitive abilities, those abilities need to be developed to be of any real value. This is no different than studying to learn a language, or putting in the time and effort to develop stronger muscles. Fortunately, the techniques for developing your intuitive abilities are fairly straightforward, requiring more time than actual effort to achieve your desired results. The following examples are a few of the more common and effective methods for strengthening your intuitive muscles.

One of the first things a person needs to do to develop intuitive abilities is to get in touch with their body. All too often, the noise and chaos filling the mind prevent an individual from hearing the message their body is sending them. Sometimes that message can come in the form of the proverbial gut feeling, but at other times, it can come in the form of sweaty palms, an increased heart rate, jitters, or any number of other physical symptoms that can serve as a warning of impending doom. To hear the message your intuition is sending, you must take the time to check how you feel physically throughout the day. This is particularly true if you are making a decision, whereby a negative physical reaction could serve as a warning to avoid a particular choice. It can also occur out of the blue, where your body just reacts to something yet to be experienced. The key is to take note of all the times your body reacts unusually. As you become more in tune with your body, you can begin to recognize the signals it is sending you, thereby using the information to avoid trouble or mistakes that can prove costly. Keeping a journal is one of the most effective ways of developing this connection. Write down any unusual feelings you get on a particular day, noting any experiences that correspond with those feelings. Eventually, you will discover the pattern between warning and reality, thus enabling you to recognize and use those warnings more effectively.

The same thing can be said concerning your inner voice. If you are the type of person who hears random statements, especially warnings or instructions, then you probably have a strong sense of clairaudience. To develop this strength, you need to start paying close attention to the messages you hear. Keeping a journal is an excellent way of developing this connection. As you write down the words you hear during a given day, you can also write down any events that occurred that might validate the message contained in those words. This will prove especially true in the event you ignore the words and suffer the consequences. As you record warnings that you ignored, along with the undesirable outcome, you will establish both a pattern and a sense of validation that will help you to listen to that voice, following its instructions more readily as you develop a strong sense of trust in it. Furthermore, this exercise will help you to distinguish between the inner voice of intuition and other random sound bites that come from your imagination or from your memory. The more time and effort you spend studying the "voices in your head", the easier it will become to tell them apart, allowing you to dismiss the junk and follow the advice of your intuition.

Finally, there is the method of strengthening your dreams. Again, keeping a journal is one of the best methods for achieving this goal. Each morning take the time to write down as much as you can remember about your dreams from the previous night. At first, you might not remember much, but as you continue the practice, you will discover your dream recall will improve exponentially. Furthermore, the intensity and frequency of your dreams will also increase, making your dreamtime that much more productive. Writing down your dreams will help you to discern the difference between those dreams that are simply fantasy-driven, as opposed to those that are, in fact, messages from your intuition. Soon you will know which dreams to listen to, and how to understand the message they are telling you. Again, it may start as a matter of trial and error where you understand the message a dream was sending after the fact. Eventually, you will begin to recognize the messages more readily, enabling you to follow them and enjoy the benefits they have to offer. This will also go a long way to developing all other clairvoyant capabilities as the development of dreams is, in essence, the development of the mind's eye.

If you still are unsure as to your inherent intuitive abilities, the best plan of attack is to try developing one at a time, taking about a month in each case. If you spend a month developing your dream recall but make little to no progress for a month, then maybe dreams aren't your thing. Try developing your inner voice next, and if that produces few to no results, then move on to clairsentience or claircognizance. In the end, everyone has a specific talent in the realm of intuitive abilities. Some may already have a good idea as to what that talent is, whereas others may have to take the time to discover it for themselves. The important thing is to remain patient and diligent, putting in the time and effort needed to achieve the results that will come as long as you stay the course.

Chapter 4: The Clairs: Clairvoyance, Clairaudience, Clairgustance, Claircognizance and Clairsentience

At the heart of all psychic abilities are five main skills or gifts. These are commonly known as the "clairs"; clairvoyance, clairaudience, clairgustance, claircognizance, and clairsentience. Most of these have already been discussed to a small degree, but this chapter will delve deeper into each, revealing their true role in the quest to discover and develop your psychic talents. Furthermore, real-life examples will be given, helping you to know whether or not you have had any experience in one or more of these areas. All in all, any psychic ability can be traced to one "clair" or another, meaning that anyone with any psychic talents can identify with at least one of the psychic abilities discussed in this chapter. Additionally, exercises and methods for development will be discussed, giving you the tools you need to raise your psychic abilities to the next level.

Clairvoyance

Of all the "clairs", the one that is probably best known to the average person is clairvoyance. Again, this is the ability to clearly see with the mind's eye, as is described by the name itself, which means "clear seeing". Although clairvoyance is a single term, there are numerous forms of clairvoyance, each unique in its own way. For example, some people can see events in other people's lives by tapping into their clairvoyant ability. This is where the image of a fortune teller using a crystal ball comes into play. While few clairvoyants actually use a crystal ball to harness their visions, the image itself is what is important. Such a person can see an image as clear as day in their mind, one that involves another person or group of people. These images can be warnings of impending danger or good omens pointing to job promotions, meeting a future spouse, or even the birth of a child. In the end, it is a bit like daydreaming about someone else's life—the only difference being that, in this case, the dream actually comes true.

Most people have experienced clairvoyance at least once in their life, whether or not they realize it. This is where the second form of clairvoyance comes into play, namely that of seeing a person in your mind that you will cross paths with in real life in the immediate future. Countless stories exist where a person sees an image of a friend or loved one, sometimes someone whom they haven't seen in a long time, only to get a phone call or surprise visit from that person during the day. A good example of this is a story where a store manager for a retail store always knew when the district manager would make a surprise visit because he would see his district manager's face either in a dream the previous night or in his mind's eye during the morning as he got ready for work. Needless to say, this gave him a huge advantage as he was always prepared before the "surprise" visit, making him look good in his boss' eyes.

Another form of clairvoyance is the ability to see a place or an event that you will come in contact with before the fact. Numerous accounts exist of people "seeing" their next house before deciding to look for another place to live. At first glance, this might not seem like an important ability; however, it can have very profound implications. While the mere fact that a person sees a house even before looking for it is amazing, the message beneath the phenomenon will, more often than not, be one of validation. In other words, knowing what your future house will look like can help you to make the right decision, turning down the other options until you find the one your intuition has prepared you for. The very same thing can happen in terms of choosing a new job, car, or even significant other. Any time you see the final outcome, you no longer have to guess at what decision to make. This ensures that you make the right decision every time.

Even so, while almost everyone has had a clairvoyant experience at one time or another, it doesn't mean that clairvoyance is everyone's personal psychic ability. The question, therefore, is how do you know if it is your personal ability? The simple answer comes down to two things: frequency and intensity. If you have had numerous experiences of seeing a person or event before it happens, even making it ordinary and mundane in your mind, then you have the knack of clairvoyance. Additionally, if your dreams are vivid, or you can imagine things in your mind with great clarity and detail, then clairvoyance is probably your gift. Once you make that determination, the next step is to develop your ability to the highest level possible.

The very first step to achieving this goal is to practice meditation regularly. You don't have to do anything elaborate; simply engage in a practice that enables you to clear your mind at the beginning and end of each day. Clearing your mind in the morning will help you to tap into your clairvoyance during the waking day, enabling you to see things before they unfold. Performing the practice at the end of the day will help you to dream better at night, giving you a clear mind that will be more open to vivid images from the spirit realm. Another proven technique for developing your clairvoyance is to keep a clairvoyant journal. In this journal, you will record all of your dreams, along with the images you receive during the regular day. Next to each vision, you will record the corresponding event that unfolds, reflecting the accuracy of your vision. The purpose of this exercise is twofold. First, it will create a sense of confidence in your ability, thereby causing you to pay more attention to the phenomenon as well as accepting the messages you are receiving. Second, it will increase your connection to your mind's eye. The more time you spend focusing on your experiences, the stronger and more frequent they will become. In the end, by ensuring that your mind is clear and by recording your visions as they occur, you will soon develop your clairvoyance to the point where you will see any event or outcome by simply tuning into your inner vision, thereby giving you an untold advantage when it comes to making the right choices and decisions every single time.

Clairaudience

The next clair to consider is that of clairaudience. As already mentioned, this is the ability to hear with the mind, hence the meaning of the name—"clear hearing". Although not as common as clairvoyance, this is another psychic phenomenon that many people all across the globe have experienced at one time or another. Simply put, this is when you hear something that could not be heard in the physical world around you. More often than not, such a sound will be a voice, usually telling you a word, number, or some other message as though someone was whispering in your ear. Unfortunately, most people dismiss such encounters as a trick of the wind or a mere figment of their imagination. Herein lies an important lesson, however. Even if such a voice were the product of a person's imagination, that does not mean that the message itself is inaccurate or unimportant. After all, what is imagination if not a form of inner dialogue? Therefore, the mechanics of clairaudience are not as important as the nature of the event itself. If you hear a voice, one that you know is not of your physical environment, you should listen to what it says regardless of its origin.

Another way that clairaudience takes shape is in the person behind the voice. Sometimes the message being conveyed isn't about the words being spoken; rather, it is about the person speaking them. Thus, if you ever thought you heard a person's voice, such as a friend or a loved one, even though that person is nowhere around, it could very well be that they are either thinking of you at that moment or in need of your help. Sometimes such an event can simply foretell of a chance encounter with that particular person later in the day, or even a phone call or email from them. The important thing to remember is that if you hear a voice that you recognize, even though that person is nowhere around, then that person is significant in the moment for one reason or another. It is up to you do discover that significance throughout the day. Whether you choose to call that person to check up on them or simply keep an eye out for them during the day, the important thing is never to dismiss such an event as you could miss out on a meaningful experience.

A good example of a real-life experience of clairaudience occurred at a funeral, where a well-loved husband and father was being laid to rest. Although the funeral took place without incident, it was after the event that things got interesting. A friend of the family had attended the funeral as a courtesy, even though he had never spent any time with the man who died. During the reception, he approached the daughter and asked what her dad called her mother, such as nicknames or the like. Dumbfounded by the question, the daughter didn't respond. At that point, the friend told her that he heard a voice at the gravesite say, "Hey, hun," as clear as day. His statement made the daughter tear up, as it turned out that it was exactly what her father called her mother all of the time.

When it comes to determining whether or not clairaudience is your skill set, the same elements apply as with clairvoyance. Namely, how often and how clearly do you hear voices? If you hear voices clearly and regularly, the chances are that you have a heightened ability when it comes to clairaudience. The next thing to do is to develop your skill set as much as possible. Fortunately, the same techniques used to develop and strengthen clairvoyance are the ones you will need for developing and strengthening clairaudience. First and foremost, you need to practice meditation regularly. After all, if your mind is filled with clutter and noise, you won't be able to hear much of anything beyond your own thoughts. However, when your mind is clear, you will hear with your inner ear just as well as you can with your physical ear. Next, you need to keep a journal in which you record every encounter. At first, some of your experiences may prove to be false readings—the consequence of the clutter filling your mind. However, after the practice of meditation begins to take hold and your focus on your inner ear increases, your encounters will become more frequent, more intense, and, most importantly, more accurate.

Clairgustance

Perhaps the least common of all the clair phenomena is that of clairgustance. Meaning "clear tasting", this is the ability to virtually taste something without having to have it in your mouth. This ability may appear completely useless at first glance—after all, what possible significance can a flavor have? However, truth be told, the sense of taste, along with smell, has been shown to be the chief senses responsible for triggering a person's memory. How many times have you eaten a piece of pie or some other home-made cooking only to recall early childhood memories of eating similar tasting foods? This doorway to the memory can be highly effective when it comes to connecting to friends or loved ones, near or far, alive or departed.

The notion that a departed soul continues to love and care for those they left behind is a common belief among countless traditions from every culture and every point in human history. Since physical speech is impossible for a departed soul, they must rely on another form of communication, one that will allow them to be seen or heard despite the veil that separates them from the living. Since taste can evoke some of the strongest memories, what better way to communicate than by putting a familiar taste in the mouth of the person they are trying to communicate with? Therefore, the next time you start tasting your long-departed grandmother's cookies, rather than simply dismissing it as a random fluke, take the time to contemplate your grandmother, even speaking to her, telling her how much you love and miss her. There is a real good chance that she is telling you the very same thing by sending you the taste of her cookies, thereby bringing her to mind.

The language of clairgustance isn't restricted to the departed. Instead, it can be just as effective when it comes to connecting to people who are still very much a part of the physical realm. If, for example, you begin to taste your mother's cooking, even though she is hundreds of miles away, it can be more than just a passing fancy—she may be thinking of you at that moment, causing you to react by experiencing a taste that brings her face to mind. Alternatively, she may need your help, or about to call or visit you. In the end, the language of taste is a bit vague in that it can't provide a clear context all of the time, such as clairvoyance or even clairaudience. Therefore, this is one skill set that really needs to be developed carefully if it is to be of any real value.

One way to improve your clairgustance ability is to keep a journal in which you record any flavors that occur seemingly out of the blue. Next to the flavor, write down the person or event that you associate it with. Finally, note any encounters that might explain the event in the first place. In other words, if you find yourself tasting your mother's food, then get a phone call or a visit from her later in the day, record those things together, allowing you to see the relationship between your psychic experience and your physical experience. If this is something you can't relate to at all, then the chances are that you don't have the knack for clairgustance. Since this is the rarest of the clair abilities, it wouldn't be surprising. However, if this is something you have experienced from time to time, then you might be one of the very few individuals who possess this ability, making it absolutely vital that you put in the time and energy needed to nurture and strengthen this rare and unique gift.

Claircognizance

Claircognizance, or "clear knowing", is probably one of the most useful of the clair abilities, enabling a person to virtually know a thing without ever having had experience or training in the area before. In fact, this is the ability that is most associated with the overall concept of intuition. One of the more commonly accepted definitions of intuition is that of an inherent knowledge—something that is understood from within rather than from without. Sometimes this knowledge comes in the form of inspiration or imagination, making a person appear to be a virtual genius with what they can produce or accomplish. Other times it comes in the form of timely knowledge, such as simply knowing to avoid a certain road at a certain time, only to find out later that an accident on that road could have proven devastating, both in terms of time and even wellbeing. In the end, the common thread is that claircognizance is the ability to know beyond what the physical senses can perceive. This gives a person untold insight into the world around them, enabling them to pursue levels of success few ever dream of.

There are many different ways in which claircognizance can manifest itself in a person's life. One way, albeit a less than desirable one, is that of a constant, nagging thought that won't go away. Sometimes this can appear as the proverbial "red flag" when you know that something just doesn't add up with regards to a situation or story. Although you can't put your finger on it at the moment, you know that there is more than meets the eye. This can often be confused with clairsentience, and the two often overlap, meaning that you might have a bad feeling about something because things don't add up. However, claircognizance goes the extra step further, enabling you to divine the answer in due course. Some refer to this as the process of germination, in which the seed of an idea virtually grows within the individual, eventually producing the solution to the problem at hand. The result is that "eureka moment" when you finally understand a particular situation, albeit from an intuitive perspective.

A good example of this is in the case of a liar. People with claircognizance will almost always be able to spot a liar because their intuition tells them there are problems with the story being told.

Again, a bad feeling may accompany this event, bridging clairsentience with claircognizance; however, the claircognizant person will eventually be able to piece together the anomalies of the story, proving the false intentions of the person involved. Another way that claircognizance takes shape is through random and seemingly unrelated thoughts or ideas just coming to mind. This isn't the same thing as the random noise that fills most people's minds; instead, it is when a person has a random thought or idea that proves significant in the immediate future. Such things as cooking extra food, only to have unexpected guests arrive during dinner, or closing the windows before leaving your house on a sunny and cloudless day, counting your blessings when you watch heavy rains appear seemingly out of nowhere. Such knowledge of events beyond the horizon is a clear sign of claircognizant abilities.

It is fairly easy to determine whether or not you are one of the many people with this particular skill set. All claircognizant people tend to have a love for problem-solving, more often than not tapping into their intuition to find solutions others would never have thought of in a million years. Additionally, claircognizant people tend to analyze things carefully, giving them the insights needed to make the best decision every time. If you can relate to these traits, you are probably claircognizant. Furthermore, if you have ever done something or made a decision that seems out of place in the moment, but that proves highly correct and valuable later on, you most likely know how to tap into your intuition and follow its lead.

Developing claircognizance is a matter of trust more than anything else. Most people with this ability have clear thoughts already—the problem is that they don't always act on those thoughts, usually because there is no logical reason to. However, more often than not, those thoughts prove themselves to be true soon enough. Not closing the windows on that sunny and clear day, only to come home to a soaking windowsill, is just one example of when that inherent knowledge proves itself infallible. The best way to build that trust is to keep a diary, one in which you record the thoughts that you have, along with whether you followed your intuition or not. Then record the results. Unfortunately, there will be times when you won't be able to prove the value of following your intuition. After all, if you don't turn down a street, thereby avoiding an accident you would have been a part of, how will you ever know? Therefore, the biggest proof will usually come when you don't follow the intuition, resulting in the negative experiences that could have otherwise been avoided.

Clairsentience

The final clair to discuss is clairsentience, or "clear feeling". This is one of the easiest clair qualities to recognize and develop. Already discussed in fairly good detail in the previous chapter, clairsentience is the psychic ability to feel your way through a given situation. As with claircognizance, the feelings may tend to be bad rather than good, pointing to the purpose of the ability. All in all, most psychic abilities serve as warnings, helping to protect you from harm or from making decisions that you will later regret. Therefore, learning to recognize the times when you have episodes of clairsentience can go a long way to improving your day-to-day life by keeping you safe and on the path to success, avoiding the twists and turns that can lead you astray.

One of the easiest ways to determine whether or not you have the gift of clairsentience is to consider how you respond when meeting people for the first time. If you are easily taken in by fake people, then you probably don't have the gift. However, if you are the type who gets a "gut feeling" about a person, usually in stark contrast to their outward appearance, then this is probably your strong suit. Again, more often than not, the feeling will be negative, warning you of the underlying danger inherent in the person you are meeting or in contact with. Even if this person appears trustworthy and decent, if you have a bad feeling about them, that feeling will prove itself right sooner or later. When you ignore the feeling and trust what your physical senses are telling you, the chances are that you will pay the price for ignoring your intuition. However, when you follow your intuition, even when it seems completely wrong, you will be the one left standing when everything comes crashing down. If you are picturing the dozen or more times this has happened to you, then congratulations—you are a clairsentient!

Needless to say, gut feelings can be caused by intuition or what you had for lunch, or a lack of sleep or any other number of conditions that can affect your physical health and wellbeing. As such, you must always remain aware of the context of your feelings, recognizing whether or not there may be other explanations less sinister than deception or impending doom. Taking a step back anytime you have a gut feeling and contemplating its true nature will almost always yield immediate answers. After all, your intuition isn't out to fool you; instead, it is out to protect you. Therefore, if you have a bad feeling come out of nowhere and you take a moment to contemplate it, if it is the result of your lunch, your mind will tell you as much, one way or another.

However, if it is more significant, you can be sure your mind will alert you to the real danger at hand. After all, the feeling isn't the message itself; rather, it is the knock on the door or the ringing of the phone. It is only intended to get your attention. The trick is to recognize it when it does, to clear your mind and accept the first thing that comes to mind when you are in that state. You might have an image of a person or an event, or you might simply know that the feeling is related to a person you are with or an event you are currently engaged in. Taking the time to pay attention to any strange feelings you have, such as gut feelings, the hair on your neck or arms standing on end, symptoms of a panic attack for no logical reason, or any other physical anomaly that is out of step with the moment, is the first step to strengthening this skill set. The more in touch you become with your feelings, the stronger those feelings will become, and the more regular their occurrence.

The next step is to begin recording events in a journal. Only by studying your feelings and the circumstances that surround them can you begin to understand their origin and meaning better. This is also a really good way of being able to distinguish from intuitive feelings as opposed to those caused by physiological conditions. Furthermore, by recording the times that you had a bad feeling about someone, who later turned out to be a danger in one way or another, will enable you to trust your feelings more and more, thereby helping you to benefit from the message they are trying to send. In the end, the value of keeping a journal simply cannot be overstated. A person who keeps a journal never struggles with their psychic abilities. Alternatively, few people who don't keep journals ever enjoy the full potential of their inherent skills. So, if you want to develop your ability, no matter what it may be, the most important thing is to keep a journal in which you record events and then go back and review them afterward in order to learn the valuable lessons they contain.

Chapter 5: Telepathy

From the Greek meaning "far away perception", telepathy is the psychic gift that enables one person to perceive the thoughts and feelings of another. Also known as "mind-reading", this gift is a fairly common one, more often associated with people who share a close bond, such as siblings or spouses. The ability for one person to finish the sentence or thought of their partner is no coincidence, nor is it the result of the two people having similar opinions. Instead, it is a sign of two people virtually sharing the same thoughts. While couples can develop telepathic abilities together, usually limited to their own thoughts and feelings, it is also possible for an individual to develop those very same abilities, enabling them to pick up on the thoughts and feelings of the people around them as well as individuals far away. This chapter will explore the science behind telepathy, as well as various ways in which telepathic abilities can be nurtured and strengthened. Furthermore, real-life examples of telepathic communication will be revealed, helping you to know whether telepathy is your personal psychic gift.

Understanding the True Nature of Telepathy

The first thing to understand about telepathy is that it is not the ability to tap into someone else's mind and read their thoughts as though you were reading a page in a book. Had this been the case, the original Greek word would have been different, using the term for "reading" rather than "perceiving". Instead, the phenomenon is based on perception, or the ability to sense another person's thoughts. Sometimes this can come in the form of the other person's thoughts appearing as your own, while other times, the origin of the particular thought is more obvious. However, the result is always the same, namely that the thought becomes your thought as well. Therefore, in a nutshell, telepathy can be seen as the ability to share thoughts, both in terms of sending thoughts to others and receiving thoughts from others.

How those thoughts manifest differs from one person to the next, being determined on how the individual's mind functions. In the case of someone gifted in clairaudience, for example, another person's thoughts can come in the form of an inner voice speaking a word or phrase. Alternatively, someone more prone to visualization will see images, whether of people, colors, objects, or even events. When two people of similar mindsets share thoughts, the results can be clearer, such as clearer images in the case of two clairvoyants, or clearer sounds in the case of two clairaudients. Fortunately, both members don't have to have similar mental qualities; rather, it simply enhances the experience.

The Science Behind the Phenomenon

Studies on the human brain have revealed numerous insights when it comes to the phenomenon of telepathy. One such insight is that the mind is designed to receive signals from outside of the body as well as from within. Professor Gregor Domes performed tests in 2007, demonstrating that certain "cues" within social interactions can be picked up by a person, allowing them virtually to know the intentions of someone else. More often than not, this plays out in the arena of dating, where certain chemistry is formed between two people interested in starting a relationship. When one person is less willing that chemistry is lacking. Although the term "chemistry" has often been used casually to describe the nature of the connection, it turns out that the term is far more accurate than most people realize. In fact, the hormone oxytocin is the main element required for receiving these social cues, proving that the chemistry in the situation is very much real.

The long-distance nature of telepathy was put to the test in 2014 when psychiatrist Charles Grau ran tests to determine whether or not the internet could be used to enhance telepathic abilities. Experiments showed that people in India were able to communicate words such as "ciao" or "hola" to people as far away as Spain by just thinking of them while being online. They did not have to type the words, say the words, or use them in any other way. Just by thinking the words clearly in their minds, they could convey them across thousands of miles to the recipients at the other end. Although this experiment could be seen to prove that certain people are highly gifted with telepathic abilities, the true revelation was the significance of the internet itself. It seems that thoughts, just like any other form of communication, can be transmitted electronically. Thus, you can think of them as radio waves, moving from one person to another. And, just like radio waves, the best way to hear the message is to be on the same wavelength as the sender, literally tuning in to their mind.

Another study conducted in 2008 served to locate the very part of the brain connected to telepathic activity. Two test subjects, one adept at telepathy, otherwise known as a mentalist, and the other a control subject with no demonstrable telepathic skill sets, were asked to draw an image based on one that had been prepared in secret. While the mentalist produced a strikingly similar image, the control subject did not. Even more telling was the fact that the parahippocampal gyrus in the mentalist was activated during the experiment, whereas it was not activated within the control subject. This definitively proved the difference between true telepathy as opposed to sheer guesswork.

While the detailed studies of professional scientists can shed a great deal of light on the nature of telepathy, it only takes a basic understanding of science to realize how telepathy actually makes sense. Again, thoughts are known to be electrical signals, just like radio waves. It is also common knowledge that water is a good conductor of electricity. This is why it's not a good idea to stand in a puddle during a lightning storm. Since the human body is comprised of about 60 percent water, it stands to reason that a person's body can act as a prime conductor of electricity, and thus, a prime conductor of thoughts. While this would explain close proximity telepathic experiences, only true psychic ability can explain the long-distance examples, meaning that telepathy can be seen as both a natural and supernatural phenomenon.

Examples of Telepathic Experiences

One of the best examples of real-life telepathic experiences can actually be found within the animal kingdom. The simple truth is that telepathy is not merely a human ability; rather, numerous animals have been found to possess the ability as well. Birds are one such example. Any time you see a flock of birds flying in formation, you will notice that the entire group can virtually turn on a dime. Thus, when the lead bird changes direction, the whole flock does as well. Needless to say, this prevents mid-air collisions that would make flying in flocks dangerous and even deadly. The question is, how do the birds know when to change direction? Telepathic communication is the answer. This is an example of close proximity telepathy, in which an individual can ascertain the intention of another. The message travels from one bird to the next in split-second timing, creating a wave pattern when the flock changes direction.

Fortunately, there are countless examples of telepathic communication within the human species as well. Some of the most amazing examples come from accounts where twins shared a similar experience, albeit unknowingly at the time. One story involves a twin who cut their heel while shaving in the shower one day. A few days later, she noticed her twin had a bandage on her heel as well. It turns out that she had gotten her first tattoo on the exact spot and at the exact time that the other twin had cut herself in the shower.

While this isn't "reading minds" per se, it demonstrates the true nature of telepathy, namely distant perception.

Another story involves twins who were still in school when they had their experience. One twin had to stay in class to take a test while the other went to get a blood test. During the test, the one boy noticed a broken blood vessel on his elbow. A few hours later, when the twins were reunited, he realized that his brother had a bandage on his elbow in the same place, the place where the needle had been injected for the blood test. Again, while this isn't about thinking the same thoughts, it is about sharing the same experience through telepathic communication. The thought process of the one was transmitted to the other, at which point the brain sent a signal to the body, causing a similar physiological reaction.

Numerous accounts exist telling of when a husband and wife send signals to each other, such as where one has an urge to stop for pizza on the way home, only to discover that the other had a craving for pizza, or where one picks up a gallon of milk not on the grocery list while at the store, only to discover that the other had spilled their milk at virtually the same moment. In the end, as compelling as these stories are, the fact remains that they are still stories, and thus they aren't as compelling as cut and dry scientific data. Fortunately, there is an undeniable trend in scientific data that demonstrates, if not outright proves, that telepathy is real. Countless experiments have been done where a person has had to guess things, such as the identity of someone sending a message or the picture on a card someone is holding, that have produced virtually the same results. When people with no telepathic abilities simply guessed at the answer, the average success rate was between twenty to twenty-five percent. Alternatively, when someone skilled in telepathy, such as a mentalist, underwent the same experiment, the success rate almost doubled, reaching as high as 43 percent. This undeniable evidence proves that telepathy is more than a gimmick; instead, it is a very real and observable phenomenon. Needless to say, if the stories mentioned earlier sound familiar, in that you have had similar experiences in your life, then it points to the fact that telepathy is your inherent psychic ability.

How to Develop your Telepathic Abilities

Many of the exercises needed to develop your telepathic abilities are the same as those needed to develop any other psychic ability. This is because the fundamental nature of all psychic abilities is largely the same, namely the ability to tap into your inner senses and understand the message those senses are telling you. Therefore, while some of the exercises listed below will seem redundant, it is only because of their absolute importance. Only when you earnestly practice such things as meditation and yoga regularly, if not daily, will your abilities begin to develop in any real and significant way. The following are a few exercises that will help you to harness and strengthen your telepathic abilities:

- **Meditation:** Again, to tap into your psychic abilities, you must gain control over your mind, specifically the amount of noise and clutter contained therein. Just as it becomes difficult to hear what another person is saying when you are in a noisy room, so too, it can be all but impossible to hear your inner voice when your mind is loud and full of chaos. Therefore, practicing relaxation meditation regularly is highly recommended, as this will help you to quiet your mind, thereby enabling you to develop a stronger connection to your inner voice. Additionally, mindfulness meditation is a good practice for developing your telepathic skill sets as this form of meditation is designed to strengthen your ability to focus on a single thought or idea, taking hold of it long enough to grasp its meaning thoroughly before letting go of it once again. For best results, it is recommended that you practice both forms together, starting with relaxation meditation to clear your mind and then moving on to mindfulness meditation to exercise your powers of perception.

The last form of meditation needed to develop your telepathic skills is that of visualization. This form will help you to strengthen your ability to envision an object, person, event, or idea with greater clarity and conviction. Since only the strongest thoughts travel well, you must think clearly and soundly if you ever want to send your thoughts to another person. This is another way in which thoughts can be seen as being similar to radio waves. Weak radio transmissions only travel over short distances and are usually hard to hear over the other noise around. In contrast, strong radio signals can travel great distances, drowning out all unwanted noise, thereby capturing the attention of the listener. By developing your visualization abilities, you will ensure that the signal you send to others is strong, clear, and powerful, thus getting the desired message through every time. All of the steps for these forms of meditation are clearly outlined in the above chapter on meditation.

• **Yoga:** It is recommended that you practice yoga as well as relaxation meditation to clear your mind and achieve the relaxed state of being needed to connect with your inner psychic abilities. In addition to deepening the relaxed state of your mind, yoga has many physiological benefits that will help to improve your telepathic abilities. One such benefit is the improved blood flow to the brain. By stretching out your muscles, you will release the tension that can reduce the flow of blood carrying oxygen to your brain, thus improving your mental clarity. The more blood your brain receives, the more oxygen it gets. Oxygen is vital for such things as clarity of thought, memory, and the ability to visualize—this is fundamental for anyone trying to develop their telepathic communication. Yoga can be practiced in conjunction with meditation or practiced on its own. The important thing is to integrate yoga into your day-to-day life in order to give yourself the best chance of success in developing any psychic skill.

- **One-on-one practice:** Since telepathy requires a minimum of two participants, this is one of the psychic skills that you can develop with the help of another. While you can choose anyone to help you in this exercise, it is recommended that you pick someone who has, at the very least, an open enough mind to believe in telepathy, and at the most, some experience of their own concerning telepathic communication. If you pick someone who doesn't believe in the process, your results will be hampered. Once you find a suitable partner, the next step is to create some exercises that will help you to hone your telepathic skills. One of the best exercises is to play the time-tested game of "Which card am I holding?" Sit at a table facing one another and have your partner draw a random card from a deck of cards. Let them stare at the card for about ten seconds, focusing strongly on what they see. As they are staring at their card, take the time to clear your mind of all thoughts, keeping it open to receive their message. Next, take it one step at a time. Don't try to see the exact card at first; instead, try to see the color. You can ask them questions, leading you to the answer. If you see red in your mind, ask them if the card is red. Next, try to see if it is a number card or a face card. These are the most significant elements of the card, so they will be the bulk of the message. If you don't see a picture, such as that of a queen, king, or jack, ask if it's a number card. If they say "yes," then go on to narrow down the specific number and the specific suit. In the end, getting half of the elements right is a sign that you are doing more than merely guessing, so don't see that as a failure. Furthermore, as time progresses, you will see your results improve as your ability increases.

Another exercise using the same setting is to reverse the roles, allowing you to act as the sender. Have the other person try to hear your thoughts on the card you are holding. After all, this is the true nature of the exercise. You aren't trying to guess the card, nor are you trying to tap into mediumship or clairvoyance in order to read the card. Instead, you are trying to hear the message the other person is sending you—or in this case, send a message to the other person. Acting as the sender will help to strengthen your ability to visualize, which can help you to see the images another person is sending you. Therefore, use both roles regularly, taking the opportunity to develop your skills as both receiver and sender. This is particularly true if you struggle reading the messages being sent to you. By switching roles, you can give yourself a break while also strengthening the skills that will enable you to receive messages more clearly and accurately.

Chapter 6: Mediumship

Mediumship is one of the more complex forms of psychic ability, consisting of numerous variations, each entailing its own unique skill sets and results. Often confused with general psychic abilities, mediumship is one of the rarer gifts found within the psychic community. This is another example where although all mediums are psychics, not all psychics are mediums. Compared to all other forms of psychic practice, mediumship is the one that works more closely with the spirit realm. This is because the very nature of mediumship requires at least one spirit guide to perform any medium-oriented activities. This chapter will explore the fascinating field of mediumship, showing how it is distinct from general psychic abilities, as well as addressing the various forms that mediumship can take. Furthermore, it will discuss how you can know if you have the necessary skill sets for practicing mediumship, as well as several methods for honing and strengthening medium abilities.

Understanding the Differences between a Medium and a Psychic

One of the biggest misunderstandings about psychic abilities is that all psychics are somehow the same. In a way, it's a bit like saying all artists are the same. Needless to say, this is obviously untrue as anyone knows that art consists of a diverse range of forms, each unique and requiring specific skills and talents. For example, you wouldn't expect an artist who paints to be able to create a sculpture from a single block of stone. Nor would you give a sculptor a set of paints and tell them to create a masterpiece. While both are artists, their talents are very different, meaning that they are not interchangeable. Psychics are the same way. A medium is not necessarily a clairvoyant, nor is a telepath necessarily a medium.

As already discussed, a psychic is someone who has a strong set of internal senses, similar to the physical senses, but not requiring physical input. However, that is generally where the similarities end. From that point forward, each different form of psychic practice takes on its own shape and requirements, making it right only for a select number of people with psychic abilities. Mediumship is a prime example of this dynamic. Although the practice of mediumship draws on some of the general psychic abilities, specifically the five clairs, it has an added dimension that sets it apart from all other psychic disciplines. That dimension is the necessity of a spirit guide. Most other psychic activities can be performed by an individual without any help from another entity. In contrast, mediumship requires another entity, making this more of a relationship than merely a practice.

The nature of this relationship can best be explained in the name itself. Mediumship comes from the root word "medium", which is defined as a channel or mode of communication. Therefore, a person who is a medium acts as a virtual radio through which a spirit conveys a message. That isn't to say that all messages are verbal; rather, they can come in many different ways, including divination, automatic writing, smoke billets, and numerous other forms of communication. In the end, the most important thing to realize is that the medium is not the source of the message; they are merely the messenger, giving voice to a departed spirit, angel, or another entity who needs to communicate with a living person.

The Different Types of Mediumship

What makes mediumship so complex is that the various forms it takes are quite different, so much so that not all mediums are capable of practicing every form. Perhaps the most common form in terms of popular culture is physical mediumship. This is often portrayed in the movies or on TV, where a medium goes into a trance and can levitate a table, much like in most depictions of a séance. While the image portrayed in popular culture tends to treat the practice of physical mediumship as a mere gimmick or party trick, the truth is far different. Physical mediums engage in their practice daily, usually in ways that enable them to gain insights into current and important issues. Divination can be seen as an example of this practice. Although an individual can practice divination in theory, most have come to believe that a spirit guide is necessary to produce accurate readings. Therefore, it is the relationship between the spirit and the medium that enables an individual to draw the right Tarot card or cast the perfect rune. The trick is that the individual yields themselves to the spirit, surrendering their will and desire in order to allow the spirit to act through them. Only then can clear communication occur, no matter what form it takes.

Another form of mediumship is known as spiritual mediumship. This form relies heavily on the five clairs, using such things as a person's ability to see, hear, feel, and know with their inner senses alone. Although a medium may choose to enter a trance-like state to achieve their goal of getting an otherworldly message, this isn't always necessary. Instead, a person can simply clear their mind to make room for the message to enter. The important thing is that the medium can set aside their personal thoughts and feelings in order to allow the message from the spirit to enter their mindfully and clearly. This is one of the main reasons why mediumship is rarer than many other forms of psychic activity. The highest level of clarity and control is needed to communicate effectively with spirits, thus requiring someone with highly advanced skills for this practice.

Before moving on to the other two forms of mediumship, it should be noted that physical and spiritual mediumship have many similarities, making them equally suited for someone with the inherent talents of mediumship. One similarity is that departed souls are often the spirit contacted for communication. Again, the iconic séance is a prime example of this activity. Whenever a person wants to contact a departed loved one, they can call on a medium to act as a bridge, conveying the message of the living person to the departed, and similarly transmitting any message that the departed soul might like to send as a response. The message from the spirit may come in the form of spoken words, an image, or even a written message in the form of automatic writing, also known as psychography, literally "psychic writing".

The next type of mediumship to explore is healing mediumship. This often comes in the form of a person laying their hands on a sick or troubled individual, thereby sending healing energy to the individual, enabling them to recover from their affliction. While this may seem like general psychic healing, the main difference is that the practitioner relies on another spirit or entity to act as the source of the energy. Thus, it isn't just the energy of the medium at work; rather, it is the energy of a spirit guide, an angel, or the Universe itself that travels through the medium and into the afflicted person. This phenomenon can be seen in many shamanic traditions where a medicine man or a healer channels supernatural energies through their body in order to heal a person—or in some cases, cast out a dark or malevolent spirit. Voodoo is another tradition that sees this practice performed regularly.

The final type of mediumship to examine is channeling mediumship. In a way, this is just like the other forms already discussed where a person channels messages, energies, or some other element to or from spirits of one form or another. However, the main difference here is that the spirit or spirits contacted are limited to only a select few. In other words, a channeling medium only communicates with specific spirits, much like a prophet communicating with a higher power. This means that such a medium would be ill-suited for performing a séance as the spirits in question there would not necessarily be the ones they have been chosen by to act as a medium for. Instead, channeling mediums are more often than not self-professed messengers of specific entities. These entities are often higher beings, such as angels or even the Supreme Deity. Alternatively, they may be entities from another dimension or realm of existence. In the end, channeling mediums are chosen by their spirit guides to perform specific functions or give specific messages. This is probably the rarest form of mediumship and the one that most people dismiss as a hoax simply because they cannot always verify the information being presented.

Some Real-Life Examples of Mediumship

Rather than providing specific examples of messages conveyed through mediumship, it would probably be more impactful to provide examples of real-life mediums, many of which you have probably already heard of but never identified as mediums. One of the best examples of a modern-day medium is Edgar Cayce. Although he referred to himself as a clairvoyant, this doesn't take away from the fact that the nature of his abilities points to him being a skilled medium. The main reason for this was the fact that he always found his messages in dreams. This reflects the trance-like state that most mediums rely on to remove their personal thoughts and desires, thereby making them more open to receiving messages from the spirit world. Also known as the "sleeping prophet", it was his religious convictions that also lend credence to his being a medium rather than merely a clairvoyant.

Another group of people to consider when it comes to real-life mediumship is prophets. Whether they are the prophets of the Old Testament, the Prophet Mohammed, or any other individual claiming to speak on behalf of God or another deity, the simple truth is that the dynamic of such communication is nothing other than mediumship. Prophets are a good example of channeling mediums, chosen to transmit messages from specific spirits and those spirits alone. Many times these people were uneducated, being picked seemingly at random to perform the task at hand. Moses himself could be considered a medium as he acted as the mouthpiece of God in the Exodus account. Regardless of whether or not you subscribe to a particular religious belief, these individuals still embody the true nature of mediumship, namely the ability to act as a bridge between the spirit world and the physical world, along which messages of varying types can flow both ways.

If scientific proof is more your speed for understanding the reality of mediumship, then the next example is ideal for you. A study in Brazil using ten test subjects was conducted to determine whether or not there was any change in brain activity during the practice of psychography, or automatic writing. Five of the subjects had been practicing for many years, whereas the other five were relative newcomers to the field. Each subject was injected with a dye that would enable brain activity to be monitored. While every subject produced a psychographic document, not all the results were the same. Those more advanced in the field showed a significant decrease in activity in the area of the brain used for focus, planning, reasoning, and the like, namely the frontal lobe regions of the brain, as compared to when they wrote ordinarily, using their own thoughts and intellect. In contrast, the newcomers demonstrated higher levels of activity in these areas, indicating an increase in focus on their part.

Despite the difference in brain activity, the one thing all ten participants shared in common was the fact that their psychographic writings were all more complex in substance and nature than their ordinary writings, something the researchers simply could not explain. According to the scientists, the ordinary writings should have been more complex as they were given the most conscious attention and focus. The fact that all ten were able to baffle researchers in this way proved that psychography is more than a hoax. Instead, it is a real phenomenon, one that proves demonstrably that something out of the ordinary truly does occur in this form of mediumship. Furthermore, the five advanced mediums should have shown far less clarity and complexity in their writings as their focus and reasoning were significantly diminished, much like it would have been after several alcoholic drinks. Inexplicably, theirs were the most complex and intelligent writings, suggesting that they truly did channel communications from the spirit realm.

Is Mediumship Right For You?

The next question to tackle is whether or not mediumship is right for you. Fortunately, there are a few telling signs when it comes to identifying a natural-born medium. One such sign is the ability to feel changes within the energy of a given area. You might feel a sudden drop in temperature or a change in the "density" of the air for no apparent reason. If this happens to you regularly, it could indicate your ability to sense spirits that are present. Furthermore, if you get images or hear messages at the same time that you sense a change in the environment, this clearly suggests that not only can you sense spirits, but you can also communicate with them easily and naturally.

Another sign you might be a medium is if you see things out of the corner of your eye. More often than not, such peripheral activities are often dismissed as a trick of the eye or shadows and the like. However, it is also possible that these occurrences are a sign that you can recognize spiritual activity in your environment. The bottom line is that any change in energy will produce a visible anomaly, one that may be too subtle for your eyes to see when focused on the area in question—much like a faint star that can only be seen by shifting your focus to the left or right of it. However, peripheral vision can often detect such anomalies as the mind is less focused on filtering the incoming signals from those parts of the eye. Therefore, if you see movement out of the corner of your eye, even when there is nothing physically there, you might be seeing the energies of the spirits around you.

Hearing messages that later turn out to be true is another telltale sign that you have mediumship capabilities. Although clairaudience is not always the result of spirit guides or entities, it can be one of the main ways a spirit chooses to communicate with a medium. This is because hearing is the second strongest sense when it comes to receiving information. Since spirits cannot be seen with the physical eye, the mind is more open to hearing a spirit, and as a result, enables a medium virtually to hear the message being delivered. Therefore, before you start thinking you have lost your mind because you hear things or see things out of the corner of your eye, consider the very real possibility that you might be a natural-born medium.

How to Develop your Mediumship Skills

If you feel that mediumship is your form of psychic ability, then the next step is to hone and strengthen your mediumship skills. Fortunately, there are several simple and proven methods for achieving this goal, each of which can be implemented into your day-to-day life quickly and easily. One of the most important methods is to engage in the practices that enable you to have a clear mind at any time. Meditation and yoga are the two main exercises that will help you to master clarity of mind; therefore, you should practice these regularly if not daily.

Another good practice is to create a ritual that helps you to get into the mood and also that enables you to close the door when you are done communicating with the spirit world. This ritual can take any form whatsoever, so be creative and expressive, choosing the setting, the activities, and the words that work best for you. For example, you might choose to burn some incense in order to focus your mind on the present moment while praying to the spirits to help you hear and understand their message to you. After your session, you can extinguish your incense and begin mindfulness meditation, helping you to focus on your physical surroundings once again.

Perhaps the most important step toward improving your mediumship skills is to practice communicating with your spirit guides. It goes without saying that any medium will have at least one spirit guide specific to them—a guardian angel, so to speak. Begin chatting with your spirit guide in the way you would a regular person. Tell them things that are on your mind, both good and bad. Begin asking for help sorting out issues, then listen for the inspiration they provide. If you are a natural-born medium, you will instantly see the results—hearing inspired words, seeing images, and knowing information as soon as you ask your question or voice your concern. Communication with your spirit guide doesn't always have to be about work; instead, you can simply chat with them, asking such things as what they look like—if they ever had a physical form. Asking their name is another excellent way to establish communication with your spirit guide. Once you hear their name, use it when talking to them, as this will help strengthen your bond. One word of warning, however; try to limit your verbal communication to times when you know you will be alone—unless you are fine with other people thinking you have lost your mind. As time progresses, you will internalize your conversations, thereby enabling you to talk to your spirit guide anywhere, anytime.

Chapter 7: Psychometry

The next psychic ability to explore is psychometry. This is the ability to ascertain specific information about an object just by holding it. In other words, someone with psychometric skills can hold a coin or piece of paper currency and see where that coin or banknote has been in the past. Needless to say, this ability is not restricted to money; instead, it can be performed with any item at all, including articles of clothing, pieces of furniture, and even houses or other buildings in general. The basic premise behind this ability is that an item absorbs a certain amount of energy from every person and event that it encounters, much like a thumbprint. Therefore, it has a memory of that person or event, and someone with psychometric abilities can tap into that memory, thereby catching a glimpse of the past, albeit recent or far back into ancient history. This chapter will discuss the specifics of psychometry, including its uses, whether or not it is the right psychic ability for you, and ways to harness and strengthen any psychometric abilities you might have. When you have finished reading this chapter, you will know whether or not psychometry is your inherent psychic ability.

What is Psychometry?

The word psychometry is Ancient Greek and roughly translates as "soul measure". This definition can have two different meanings. On the one hand, the "psych" portion of the word can refer to the fact that psychometry is a psychic gift, one that is performed with your inner senses as opposed to your five physical senses. However, on the other hand, it can also indicate that what you are measuring is the energy of the object itself. This, in essence, suggests that you are tapping into the very soul of a particular object or place, much like telepathy is tapping into the mind of another person. Whether you believe that objects have souls or they simply accumulate residual energy is of little consequence. The bottom line is that a person with psychometric abilities can read the energy an object contains.

Again, a good way to envision this is to imagine that every person that touches an object leaves a small amount of their energy on that object, much like they leave behind their fingerprints when touching that object. And, just as fingerprints can be used to identify a person, so too can the residual energy left behind on an object. This is particularly true in the case of an object that is used by the same person regularly. Something like a hairbrush, wallet, or pair of glasses can contain a huge amount of residual energy from a single individual, making it easy for someone with psychometric skills to get a clear image of who that person is/was. Furthermore, items associated with specific events, such as sporting equipment or military equipment, can possess the energy of an event, allowing a psychometric expert to see a touchdown being scored just by holding the game's winning ball.

Perhaps a better way to imagine it is to think of the residual energy as a snapshot, a single image reflecting where that object has been. Someone with psychometric skills can literally read the images contained in an object, thereby seeing the history of the object. This is where things can get a bit dangerous though. For example, weapons such as bayonets or swords may contain the image of the brutal slaying of an enemy combatant. Likewise, buildings such as hospitals or prisons may contain residual energy of a negative nature, making for bad reading when it comes to the images presented. Therefore, it is always vital to choose the objects you will read with great care as the images they contain can be anything at all—from the most wonderful to the most horrifying. Additionally, it is commonly accepted that the more intense a situation is, the more energy that situation creates. Therefore, items may have clearer images of more negative events as those are usually the ones that create the most intense energy. This makes it all the more important to choose the objects you read with great care.

How You Can Tell if Psychometry is Right for You

When it comes to determining whether or not you have psychometric skills, this too can be an exercise fairly negative in nature. The reason for this is that most of the telltale signs of psychometric abilities are stressful and unpleasant, often causing a person great distress. One such example is if you feel overwhelmed or oppressed whenever you are in an antique store. While many people can spend hours looking at all the wonderful and mysterious relics from the past, anyone with psychometric abilities will tend to become depressed and even anxious in such a place. This is because all of the residual energy in the objects present will overwhelm their senses, much like hundreds of radios being turned on at once. Therefore, if you feel uncomfortable whenever you are around old items, especially in the case of being in an antique store or a thrift shop, then you are probably a good fit for psychometry.

Another way to know if you possess psychometry skills is if you feel heavy or sad in older buildings. Again, places such as hospitals, prisons, or any other place where the energy would be highly negative will doubtlessly have an impact on almost any psychic, even those without inherent psychometric talents or skills. However, if ordinary places such as old houses, railway stations, or even old buildings turned into restaurants cause you depression, fatigue, or even anxiety, then you are probably someone with natural psychometric abilities. Not being comfortable in second-hand clothing, using old furniture, and other such issues with anything that has been used before is almost always a clear sign of psychometric abilities.

The feelings you get from old places, or old objects, don't always have to be negative, however, to indicate psychometric skills. This comes down to the simple fact that empathy is at the heart of psychometry. Thus, when an empath can control the flow of information coming in, they can avoid the negative impact of such places as antique stores and the like. This is because they don't become overwhelmed by the energy surrounding them. As a result, rather than becoming stressed or fatigued, they can simply feel the energy around them, much like hearing the ambient sound of numerous conversations in a restaurant. Therefore, if old places feel different to you, or old objects have a quality that sets them apart from new ones, psychometry is probably right for you.

Real-life Applications of Psychometry

As with any other psychic ability, psychometry can have some very useful real-life applications. That said, those applications will be far fewer than the ones associated with a talent, such as telepathy, where real-time information can be obtained, helping a person make the best decisions and choices every time. Nevertheless, psychometry can prove more useful than a mere talking point at parties. One way that psychometry can be put to use is in the area of antiques themselves. Forgeries and fakes are commonplace in the antique market, providing a lucrative business for those who can pass off such fakes to would-be buyers. However, a person with psychometric abilities will be able to tell the difference between a real antique and a fake just by the energy signature of the item. No matter how old an object looks, if it is relatively new, it will lack the depth of energy that a true antique possesses. Even the most novice practitioner of psychometry can tell a new item from an old item just by holding it for a few seconds.

Another application, perhaps one more likely to occur in day-to-day life, is in the area of identifying the owner of lost objects. While a lost purse or wallet will usually contain a photo ID of the owner, things like keys, a phone, or a jacket won't. This means it can be all but impossible to know whom to look for if you spot a set of keys laying on a picnic table or chair in a restaurant. However, if you have psychometric abilities, you will hold that item for a moment and catch a glimpse of the person it belongs to. At the very least, you will know if it is a man or a woman, someone old or young, and hopefully, you will even be able to see the color of their hair. This can make all the difference when searching the nearby crowd to see whom the keys might belong to. Needless to say, when you see someone matching the image in your mind looking around as though they lost something, you can be sure they will appreciate you returning their keys or phone to them.

Equally as important as knowing how psychometry can be used in real life, so too, you must know its limitations. Unfortunately, television and movies often depict psychometry in a very unreal and irrational way. This is particularly true in any situation where a telepath holds a murder weapon in order to identify the murderer. There are several things wrong with this depiction, not least of which is the fact that no law enforcement agency would ever base an investigation on such a tip. Furthermore, this idea significantly underestimates the impact of the images that a telepath can see from an item. Not only would images from a murder weapon be devastating to your heart and mind, but the energy itself, full of horror and pain, would be immeasurably traumatizing. Therefore, no sane person would ever willingly use their psychometric skills in conjunction with a murder weapon, a torture device, or any other object knowingly used to create pain and suffering on another living being.

How to Develop your Psychometric Skills

As with any skill or talent, the best way to improve your psychometric skills is with practice, practice, and even more practice. Fortunately, the process for conducting a psychometric reading is very straight forward, requiring only five steps to accomplish. This means that you can practice virtually anytime, anywhere, and as often as you like. The following are the basic steps of a psychometric reading:

- *Step one:* Wash and dry your hands thoroughly before handling an object. This will remove any dirt that might interfere with the reading, as well as any residual energy left from handling a previous object. If you can't wash your hands, simply wipe them a few times on your pants leg, just enough to brush off any surface residue.
- *Step two:* Rub your hands together vigorously for about ten seconds. This will generate energy in your palms and fingertips. The more energy you have in your hands, the easier it will be to absorb energy from the object. A good way to know if you are ready is to hold your hands together after rubbing, slowly separating them to about a quarter of an inch apart. If you can feel a tingling sensation or a resistance to pulling them apart, you know you have generated the energy you need. If you don't feel anything, rub them for another ten seconds and try again.
- *Step three:* Pick up an object and hold it in your hands. If you are a beginner, it is recommended that you start with an object that would have been used daily, such as glasses, a hairbrush, or a set of keys. Not knowing the owner can also be useful as it will prevent your mind from conjuring up memories of the person, such as a friend or a loved one. This will ensure that any images you see are the result of the object and not your memory or imagination.
- *Step four:* Close your eyes and relax. Imagine you are waiting for the object to speak to you. Listen to what it is saying, clearing your mind, and focusing on anything you see or hear. Let the object do the talking. The quieter your mind, the better your chances will be of having a successful reading. You might want to take a couple of deep breaths first just to help you relax and clear your mind, bringing your attention to the moment at hand.
- *Step five:* Be receptive. One mistake beginners often make is rejecting images they think don't make sense. Remember, you have no idea where this object has been, so take the

images you see as fact. Furthermore, always grab on to the first image that comes to mind. This will be the most accurate as your mind hasn't had a chance to judge that image or alter it in any way. As you practice, you will develop a more receptive mind, one that accepts whatever it sees and hears without doubt or hesitation. Then you will be able to perform this task with greater confidence in the results you get, enabling you to see glimpses into the past wherever you go simply by opening your mind and allowing the objects to tell their story.

At first, your results may be random, at best, being about half accurate and half inaccurate. However, as you continue to practice, you will find that your accuracy levels will rise, eventually reaching as high as 85 to 90 percent, as is often the result with highly adept individuals when tested under laboratory conditions. Perhaps the most important thing to remember is that the ability of psychometry is to be enjoyed, so make it fun for yourself. Who knows, eventually you may be able to touch an old building and get a snapshot of what the town looked like 100 or even 200 years ago. You might even see the people who were present at the time. If you get good enough, you might even be able to hear what they were saying. After all, you will be one of the lucky ones who will know what it's like when the walls can actually talk!

Chapter 8: Aura Reading

One of the most hotly debated topics within the psychic community, as well as within the scientific community, is that of auras. Mystics and spiritual traditions have promoted the existence of auras for millennia, covering just about every culture across the globe. Despite the widespread belief in auras, many still dismiss their existence because most people cannot see them. Recent scientific studies have revealed that auras can, in fact, exist, giving credence to the ancient traditions. However, despite their findings, many scientists still debate the nature of auras and the significance they hold. Regardless of this ongoing debate, many people crave the ability to see and interpret the auras of people around them. This chapter will provide the tools needed for seeing auras, as well as insights regarding the true nature of auras and the meaning behind the different forms and colors they can take. Additionally, the role that chakras play concerning auras will also be discussed, along with how to read and interpret the color of each different chakra.

A Basic Overview of Auras

In most spiritual traditions, the nature and appearance of auras are largely the same. A person's aura is the energy that surrounds their body, forming a sort of envelope or bubble of pulsating, glowing energy that reflects their physical, emotional, and mental state of being. Sick people, for example, will have darker, less vibrant auras, some of which even seem incomplete with holes or areas missing. In contrast, healthy, happy people will have brighter auras, usually yellow or white, extending as far as three or four feet from their body, creating a virtual bubble of energy that shields them from negative energy in their surroundings.

Although the basic elements of an aura are largely agreed upon in terms of their size, their vibrancy, and the impact of positive and negative forces upon them, there are a few debates within psychic circles regarding the meaning of their colors. Some schools of thought claim that auras can contain the same colors as chakras with each meaning something similar if not exactly the same as their chakra counterpart. However, other traditions hold that there are fewer colors and that these colors hold a completely different meaning. A perfect example is the color red. While some traditions claim that red indicates sexuality, assertiveness, and a competitive nature, others suggest that it reflects anger or high levels of stress. Subsequently, context is all-important when it comes to interpreting the colors of auras as red may indicate that the individual is strong-willed, or rage-driven, and thus should be kept at a safe distance.

As already mentioned, numerous scientific studies have concluded that auras do, in fact, exist. However, these studies do little to support the idea that different colors represent different psychic abilities or spiritual qualities. Instead, the basic belief within the scientific community is that auras are nothing more than the electromagnetic field surrounding a living being. This is what is referred to as the Bio-Energetic Field within the scientific community. The different functions of the human body, such as circulation, digestion, and respiration, all create electrical impulses that travel throughout the body. Furthermore, these impulses create electrochemical reactions throughout the nervous system. Subsequently, when a person is in peak health, where all of these functions are operating at their highest levels, then there is a tremendous amount of electrical activity taking place all through the body, creating a halo effect around the individual. The healthier and more vibrant the individual is the brighter their bio-energetic field. When a person is ill or has suffered trauma, this field is reduced, both in size and intensity.

While science believes that an aura is largely one layer of energy produced by the electrochemical activities within the body, certain spiritual traditions believe that there are as many as seven separate layers of an aura, each representing a unique quality or condition of the individual. These seven layers of the aura are as follows:

- *Layer one: Etheric*. This layer is the one closest to the body and is usually the easiest to see. Associated with the root chakra, it represents a person's physical health and wellbeing and is bright blue when the individual is in good health. Physically active people tend to have the brightest etheric layers.
- *Layer two: Emotional.* The emotional layer surrounds the etheric layer and is connected to a person's emotional wellbeing. Associated with the solar plexus chakra, it can be any color in appearance—the brighter the color, the healthier the person. When the colors are dark or muted, it represents stress, fatigue, or generally poor emotional health.
- *Layer three: Mental.* The mental layer is the third from the body and is associated with a person's mental health and wellbeing. Associated with the sacral chakra, this layer is bright yellow when in good health. Due to the mental nature of this level, it is easiest to see around the head and neck area and is most vibrant in creative people and intellects.
- *Layer four: Astral.* This level is the fourth from the body and is associated with the heart chakra. Representing the interpersonal relationships of an individual, it is pink or rosy red, most vibrant among those with loving personalities,

whereas it can be subtle or even absent in introverts or those suffering heartbreak or depression.

- *Layer five: Etheric Double.* The etheric double layer is associated with the throat chakra and is the layer that represents your true self. This is another layer that can contain any color, depending on the qualities of the individual. When a person is living a life per their true nature, this level will be most vibrant; however, someone who is disconnected from their true identity will have a muted fifth layer.
- *Layer six: Celestial.* Representing unconditional love and connection with all living things, this level is pearl-white and associated with the third eye chakra. Psychics and other spiritually-minded individuals display strong celestial layers.
- *Layer seven: Ketheric Template.* As the last layer, this is the one furthest from a person's physical body, reaching an estimated three feet. Associated with the crown chakra, this layer is gold in color and has the highest frequency vibration. It is considered the embodiment of a person's immortal soul; thus, it reflects the wellbeing of the individual across all incarnations. It also reflects the strength of a person's connection to the divine source.

Interpreting the Different Colors

As already mentioned, there are two main schools regarding the different colors of the aura and their meaning. For this book, the more common interpretation will be used, specifically that associated with the colors of the chakras. The following are the colors of the aura and their meanings:

- **Dark red:** Someone with a dark red aura will generally be hardworking, energetic, and active.
- **Bright red:** A bright red aura points to someone who has a highly competitive spirit, strives to win at whatever they do

and is usually sexually assertive, harnessing raw, primal energy.
- **Orange:** A person with an orange aura is usually very business-minded, capable of handling facts and figures, as well as being good with people. They can also prove adventurous in nature, such as an entrepreneur.
- **Bright orange/yellow-orange:** This color points to someone with an academic nature, given to logic and deep thinking.
- **Yellow:** As the color might suggest, a yellow aura represents someone bright and sunny in disposition, spontaneous and expressive.
- **Bright Green:** People with bright green auras are generally social, given to community activities and occupations, such as teaching or daycare.
- **Dark Green:** A dark green aura suggests someone who is good at organizing and being goal-oriented.
- **Blue:** This color signifies a person who is sensitive to others and is a loyal and caring friend.
- **Indigo:** A person with an indigo aura is usually more introverted, preferring solitude and tranquility. As a result, they are usually calm and clearheaded, often showing artistic qualities.
- **Violet**: A violet aura can be found in people who are charismatic, often with a sensual personality, and who can easily make connections with others.
- **Lavender:** Highly sensitive, even to the point of being fragile, lavender aura people are very imaginative and in touch with higher levels of consciousness.
- **White:** This is the highest color, representing transcendence, spirituality, and a unity of body and mind.

One of the main things to look for, in addition to the color itself, is the brightness of the aura. When a person is healthy, happy, and in tune with their inner, true nature, their aura will be brighter and more vibrant. In contrast, someone who is depressed, ill, or suffering inner conflict will have a muted aura, sometimes even brown, representing the dark, dreary condition of their energy.

Chakras and Cleansing Techniques

Although chakras are separate from auras, they are closely related, influencing the strength and clarity of the aura itself. When chakras are balanced and unblocked, flowing naturally and strongly, a person's aura will be more vibrant and balanced. Alternatively, when chakras are blocked or out of balance, the aura will suffer, becoming smaller and more muted in appearance. Fortunately, by understanding chakras, their meanings, and how to manage them, you will maintain good chakra health, thus promoting a strong and healthy aura. The following is a list of the seven chakras, revealing their significance and the location of each within the physical body:

- Root Chakra: This is the lowest of the seven chakras, located at the base of the spine. Its color is red, and it represents being down to earth, raw energy, and physical activity.
- Sacral Chakra: The second of the chakras, located just below the navel, is orange. It is associated with creativity and procreation, giving life in all forms.
- Solar Plexus Chakra: Yellow in color, this chakra represents a person's ability to assimilate to new conditions. It also points to motivation and being goal-oriented. Located in the stomach region, it also affects healthy digestion.
- Heart Chakra: Located in the center of the chest, this chakra is green and represents love, relationships, and the awareness of one's soul.
- Throat Chakra: As the name suggests, this chakra is located in the base of the throat. Blue in color, it affects communication, specifically verbal communication.
- Third Eye Chakra: The most commonly known of all chakras, the third eye chakra is located in the forehead, just

above the level of the physical eyes. Indigo in color, this chakra represents intuition and insight.

- <u>Crown Chakra:</u> The last and highest of the chakras, the crown chakra is associated with peace, wisdom, and spirituality. Violet in color, it is located at the top of the head, just above the crown.

When balanced, each of the seven chakras serves to create, attract, or direct energy to different parts of the body. However, even when balanced and healthy, some chakras will tend to be stronger and more pronounced within an individual, creating specific characteristics that define the person. Someone with a strong throat chakra, for example, will be more adept at giving speeches or just verbal communication in general. The extra strong nature of the throat chakra may affect the overall color of their aura, giving it a blue hue reflecting the nature of the energy itself.

Keeping the chakras balanced and unblocked is a critical step toward maintaining good chakra health as well as good mental, emotional, and even physical health. Fortunately, there are a few simple techniques for ensuring that the chakras operate at peak efficiency, providing the energy needed to keep you at your physical and spiritual best. The techniques can be broken down into physical and non-physical, each providing a different approach to maintaining optimum chakra health.

Yoga is by far the most effective physical technique for keeping chakras open and strong. The act of stretching the body ensures that energy flows throughout unimpeded, thus increasing the health and wellbeing of all chakras and the functions they support. The relaxation element of yoga also helps reduce stress, making yoga a bit of a hybrid, combining the physical and non-physical elements into a single regimen.

Maintaining a proper diet is another physical technique for increasing chakra health. Processed foods, fried foods, and anything high in sugar content will make the body sluggish, filling it with toxins that impact the health of the chakras. Alternatively, fresh fruits, vegetables, and other healthy foods serve to provide energy to the body while cleansing it of toxins and other harmful elements. The result is greater chakra health, resulting in a more vibrant aura.

Meditation is one of the non-physical techniques to help improve chakra health. Although meditation can be a physical act, it is the mental aspect of it that affects chakra health and wellbeing. In short, the reduction of stress helps open chakras, allowing energy to flow naturally and in high quantities. The better your energy flow, the better your physical and emotional health and wellbeing. Therefore, if you want to improve the performance of your chakras, make sure to make meditation a part of your regular routine.

Finally, avoiding stress in any way possible is the key to maintaining good, strong chakra health. Taking the time to sit in a peaceful, tranquil environment regularly will go a long way to preventing the buildup of stress that can block and even shut down chakras, creating a seriously negative impact on your energy. Additionally, avoiding stressful situations can go a long way to protecting your chakras from the harm that stress can cause. In the end, all of the things that help to create and maintain a healthy state of mind will also help to create and maintain the best levels of chakra health.

How to Develop your Ability to Read Auras

Now that you know what auras are, what their colors mean, and the impact that chakras have on them, the final step is to develop your ability to read auras. As with all other psychic abilities, reading auras may not be right for everyone. In theory, any person can develop any psychic ability, at least to some level. However, the best approach is to discover the ability that is inherent to you and develop that to its greatest potential. The very same thing holds true for reading auras. If you aren't a natural in this particular skill set, you may find success elusive.

Fortunately, it is fairly easy to know whether you have the potential to read auras. One sign that you are gifted in this area is the ability to feel another person's energy. If you can't feel someone else's energy, the chances are that you will never be able to see it. It's all a matter of sensitivity. Thus, if you feel uneasy around someone who is a threat, or you feel at peace around someone who can be trusted, then you can clearly sense their energy. With practice, you should be able to translate the ability to feel energy into the ability to see energy.

Another signal that you might have the ability to see auras is if you often see things in your peripheral vision. This has already been discussed in reference to sensing spirits that are present. If you see shadows, motions, or other anomalies out of the corner of your eye, even when nothing is there, you will probably have an easy time seeing auras. The main reason for this is that auras are often best seen out of the periphery where the mind can't filter them out. Additionally, the subtle nature of auras can make them hard to see a face on them, much like a faint star in the night sky. If you relate to one or all of these skill sets, then practicing the following techniques for reading auras should enable you to have your first experience in no time.

The first step to reading auras is to develop your sense of clairsentience. This is when you feel the energy of the people around you. Start to pay close attention to how you feel when you are around certain people. If you feel uncomfortable around someone, take the time to see if they are angry or just negative in general. This doesn't necessarily mean that the individual is a bad person; rather, it can indicate that they are simply in a bad mood. Alternatively, if you feel good around someone, such as happy or safe, take the time to see what mood they are in to confirm your feelings. The more accurate your clairsentience is, the easier it will be to see auras.

The next step is to develop your peripheral vision. A good way to do this is to focus on a single point in the room for about a minute. Allow your eyes to go slightly out of focus so that you don't strain them by staring at one thing for too long. Once you have softened your focus, start observing the objects or people outside your direct line of sight. See how much detail you can make out while keeping your eyes fixed on the one spot. This will sharpen your ability to recognize things out of your normal range of view. As mentioned before, auras can usually be more easily seen when not focused on directly, so developing a strong peripheral vision is critical for reading auras.

Sensing color is the next step in developing the ability to see and read auras. This can be done by placing sheets of colored paper on a wall. The colors should represent the colors of the aura, or chakras, as you want to focus specifically on being able to see those more than any colors in general. Practice on one color at a time. Take note of how that color makes you feel when you see it. This will help connect your ability to feel energy with your ability to see a person's aura. Additionally, practice seeing the sheets of paper out of your peripheral vision. This will develop your ability to see color outside your focused line of sight. You can take one day or even one week per color, depending on how quickly you feel your senses are developing.

The final phase for developing the ability to see and read auras is to practice on a friend. Have your friend sit across from you in a low-lit room. Avoid windows, as daylight can create color fluctuations in the room. Also, have them wear neutral colors, even black, as this will make the colors of their aura pop out more, making it easier for you to see. For best results, you can have them stand in front of a neutral-colored wall, about fifteen inches from you. Once in place, begin to focus on the wall next to them, about a couple inches from their body. As you focus, take note of your feelings. Do you feel happy, sad, nervous, or something else? When you determine the feel of their energy, you know what color to look for. Allow your focus to soften; thus, bringing your attention to your periphery vision. At this point, you must remain open-minded. If you think you see a color, any color at all, accept it. Don't question it, don't dismiss it, and don't look for something different. By accepting what you see, you open your mind and senses to the experience, thereby increasing your ability to see their aura. The more you practice this technique, the easier seeing auras will become. Eventually, you will see them anywhere at any time, regardless of environmental conditions.

Chapter 9: Healing

If you ask the average person on the street what superpower they would most like to have, you will hear a wide range of answers. Many would choose to fly, be super strong, or be able to access unlimited knowledge. A select few, in contrast, would choose to be able to heal people, mostly just by touching them. While this sounds about as unlikely a power to achieve as the ability to fly or punch through stone walls, the fact is that healing is another psychic ability, one that thousands of people possess all around the world. Unfortunately, few of these people are even aware of their gift, and fewer still know how to harness it, strengthen it, and put it to good use. This chapter will discuss several forms of psychic healing, showing how it is very much a part of holistic medicine in the modern world. Additionally, it will reveal how to determine whether or not you are a born healer, one gifted with the skill sets needed to be able to heal a person with a single touch. Finally, it will discuss how to strengthen your inherent skills, thus enabling you to have the healing effect on the world that you so desperately crave.

What is Psychic Healing?

The first thing to explore is the true nature of psychic healing. While most people turn to physical sources, such as doctors and over the counter medicines, when they get sick, some prefer a more spiritual approach, one that taps into the healing power of energy. Physical treatments heal a person from the outside; in contrast, psychic healing brings health and wellbeing from within, healing the individual at the very root of the problem, not merely treating the symptoms. This system is based on one simple truth: namely, that a person's physical, mental, and emotional health and wellbeing are all affected by the condition of their energy. When a person's energies are out of balance or blocked, physical and emotional illness will result. Thus, psychic healing is the practice of restoring proper balance and flow to a person's energies, thereby healing all sickness and suffering by fixing the actual cause on the spirit level.

There are numerous forms of psychic healing, each with their own unique methods and techniques for achieving the ultimate goal of total health and wellbeing. While some focus on a general approach, such as channeling the Universal life force into a person to recharge their energies, others have a more fine-tuned approach, focusing on the role of chakras and their performance when it comes to producing and maintaining energy. Subsequently, numerous tools and practices can be employed, each forming a specific tradition within the overall scope of psychic healing. This creates the same situation as that found in mediumship—namely, that not all psychic healers can practice all forms of psychic healing. Therefore, it is not only vital to discover whether or not you have the skill sets required for psychic healing in general, but it is also necessary to discover exactly what type of psychic healing is right for you.

Signs that you are a Psychic Healer

As with all psychic abilities, everyone has the potential to achieve some level of skill in this practice. However, those lacking inherent skills will struggle to produce even the most menial of results. Therefore, this is not a psychic ability recommended for just anyone. It is one that should only be pursued by an individual who demonstrates the qualities necessary for attracting and channeling healing energies in a significant and meaningful way. Fortunately, the signs for these qualities are easy to spot, making it easy to determine if psychic healing is your inherent gift. The following is a list of signs that will determine whether or not you have the traits of a natural-born healer:

1. You tend to feel deep empathy for others.
2. People close to you tend to remain in good overall health.
3. People tend to confide in you concerning their problems and pains.
4. Children and animals feel safe around you, even when they are skittish around other people.
5. You prefer to spend time alone in peaceful settings.
6. You are highly sensitive to the feelings and suffering of others.
7. Your dreams convey messages regarding sickness or healing in your body.
8. More than anything, you desire to help and heal others in any way possible.
9. You prefer spending time in nature, away from the hustle and bustle of humanity.
10. You prefer to listen to others rather than speak.
11. You have a deep interest in spirituality and have experienced events of awakening from time to time.
12. Medications and drugs don't often affect you the same way they affect others.
13. You have healers in your family, such as parents or grandparents.

If you identify with half or more of these statements, then the chances are that you are a natural-born healer. The next step is to identify the different types of healing so that you know which path to follow in your quest to develop your inherent skills.

The Role of Energy in Psychic Healing

As already mentioned, energy plays a huge role, both in terms of illness as well as psychic healing. Only when you understand the significance of energy can you begin to hone your abilities, thereby developing the healing touch you were meant to have. It should be mentioned again that sickness and distress are caused by an imbalance of energy in the individual. Sometimes this imbalance can be the result of physical trauma; however, more often than not, it is the result of emotional or spiritual trauma. Stress, for example, can significantly hinder the efficiency of chakras, thus reducing the flow of energy within a person's body. This will lead to such things as sore muscles, low levels of physical energy, and the increased likelihood of becoming ill. Rather than addressing those symptoms with traditional medicines and treatments, psychic healers know that the best way is to restore the balance and flow of energy within the patient, thereby restoring their natural ability to eliminate sickness and disease.

The main way that the energy of the patient is restored is by channeling healing energies into their body. This can come in two forms. First, the healer can use his or her own energy, often referred to as "ki" or "prana", to help boost the energy levels of the patient, much like jump-starting a car with a dead battery. By sending their energy into the patient, a healer can restore the patient's energy to a level where they will be able to return to a normal state of health and wellbeing. The downside of this is that the healer will become depleted if they have patients needing large amounts of energy in order to recover or in the case where they treat multiple patients within a given period. Subsequently, a healer must take the time to recharge their own energies in between sessions to ensure their own health and wellbeing.

The second form of energy healing is that of channeling, where the healer draws not from their personal energy, but rather from the healing energy of the Universe itself. In this case, the healer acts much like a medium, but instead of channeling a message from a spirit, they channel energy from the Universe. In a way, they act as an extension cord, connecting the patient with the source of energy that will restore their health and wellbeing. The positive side to this form is that it doesn't draw on the energy of the healer, meaning it won't deplete the healer's energy levels in the process. Furthermore, some techniques make it possible for the patient to channel the energy themselves, thereby enabling them to act as their own healer.

Common Forms of Psychic Healing

Just as there are many different specialties within the medical field, each focusing on a specific form of health and recovery, so too, there are several types of psychic healing. Each of the types can be classified into three categories. The first is what is known as Spiritual Healing. This is when a healer invokes the energies of the Universe to enter the body of the patient, thereby restoring the individual's energy levels, and thus their health and wellbeing. An example of Spiritual Healing is Reiki, an Ancient Japanese healing technique in which the healer channels ki energy to the patient, using their hands as the outlet for that energy. Some practitioners place their hands directly on the patient, while others keep them several inches over the patient's body. The name Reiki comes from the Japanese meaning Universal Power (Rei) and Energy (ki), signifying the source of the healing energy the practitioner channels to the patient.

Another type of Spiritual Healing is the use of crystals for restoring the energy levels in a patient. This practice focuses on restoring energy to the chakras, using the unique crystal associated with the specific chakra. For example, if a person has a throat issue, or is having trouble speaking, then their throat chakra needs to have its energies restored. Crystals such as aquamarine or sodalite will be placed on the patient to attract the necessary frequency of energy.

The blue color of the crystals reflects the blue color of the chakra, and thus the frequency of the energy associated with it. The advantage of this practice is that the healer doesn't need to act as a channel for the energy to travel through, so there is no wear and tear on them as such. Additionally, the patient can actually perform the healing act themselves if they know what crystals to use for the chakra needing to be restored.

The second category of psychic healing is Pranic Healing. Originating in India, this form of healing incorporates the life force of the healer, otherwise known as the ki or the Prana. Unlike Spiritual Healing, which uses the life force of the Universe, this is where the healer will use their energy, much like the example mentioned above regarding jump-starting a car. Quantum Healing is an example of Pranic Healing. This is where the healer uses specific techniques to increase their own Prana, thereby enabling them to provide the energy necessary to restore the patient to health. Breathing techniques, body awareness techniques, and a special awareness of the different frequencies of energy come into play, allowing the healer to know which energies need restoring and how to increase those energies within themselves. They also know what symptoms to look for when determining deficient energies, much like a doctor would use physical symptoms to diagnose a disease.

The third category of psychic healing is Mental Healing. This is where the healer uses their mind to both diagnose and treat the patient. In a way, this is almost a form of telepathic healing, whereby the healer taps into the subconscious of the patient in order to determine the nature of the illness and then uses their mind to envision the healing process, sending that image into the subconscious of the patient like a program of sorts. When done correctly, the healer can virtually instruct the patient to get better just by using their telepathic abilities. Needless to say, this is the rarest of the three categories, requiring the highest levels of intuition, telepathy, and clairvoyance that a person can achieve.

Two other methods of healing focus more on the correction of energy flow rather than the introduction of healing energy. These are the Chinese forms of healing known as acupuncture and acupressure. Acupuncture is the practice of using special needles to draw out negative energy that blocks the flow of healthy energy throughout the body. It focuses on the fourteen meridians of energy flow, discovering where blockages are located and releasing those blockages through the needles. While this practice looks painful, the patient barely feels the needles at all. Instead, they feel the release of tension, which restores proper energy flow to their body once again.

Acupressure acts in much the same way, except that it utilizes pressure instead of needles. The healer will use his or her fingers to apply pressure to the affected parts of the body, thus releasing tension and restoring proper energy flow to the patient. Needless to say, in both cases, the healer has to have the intuition needed to know where the blockages are, as well as how to release them. Still, where these treatments differ is that the healer does not send energy into the patient; rather, they release the patient's energy, thereby restoring overall health and wellbeing to the individual.

How to Develop your Psychic Healing Skills

When it comes to developing your healing skills, the best method is practice, practice, and more practice. Of course, the first step is determining which type of psychic healing is best for you. To do this, you want to find practitioners from each discipline and talk to them about your desire to become a healer. These people will know what it takes to perform their specific variety of psychic healing, so they will be able to tell whether you are a good fit or not. Furthermore, they will take you under their wing and teach you the ropes, further testing your natural abilities. If you struggle to make progress in one particular discipline, it might mean you need to try another. Eventually, you will find your niche, feeling your skills rise within you as you begin to learn and develop the techniques of the healing form that is right for you.

Chapter 10: Contacting and Communicating with your Spirit Guides

The final and perhaps most exciting psychic ability to explore is communicating with spirit guides. While all psychic abilities are amazing and wonderful, communicating with spirit guides takes the psychic experience to the next level, literally. Spirit guides have been a part of human culture since prehistoric times, with shamanic practices still relying on the knowledge and insights of spirits in many African and South American cultures to this very day. Even the major religions of the world, including Judaism, Islam, and Christianity, contain rich and varied traditions when it comes to spirit guides and the forms they can take. The bottom line is that just about every spiritual tradition believes that spirits exist to help and guide people through every aspect of their Earthly existence.

Unfortunately, many people fail to recognize the messages their guides are trying to send them, resulting in them blindly making their way through life, making needless mistakes and missing countless opportunities. For those who discover and listen to those messages, the results are vastly different. Those are the people who can avoid most pitfalls and know when to embark on new and exciting adventures. This chapter will discuss the different types of spirit guides that exist, helping you to recognize those sent to help you along your path. Furthermore, it will reveal ways to discover and contact your personal guides, creating a rich and meaningful relationship with them—one that will change your life in ways most people can't even imagine.

What are Spirit Guides?

The first thing to address is the true nature of spirit guides. Perhaps the best way to explain what they are is to consider one of the most common images of them in use today, specifically that of an angel. The word "angel" comes from the Ancient Greek word "angelos", which translates as a messenger. This dismisses the idea that angels are fat babies rolling around in clouds, or harp loving musicians passing the time singing in long white robes while humanity struggles far below. As messengers, angels are spirits that not only observe humanity closely, but also try to give advice, warnings, and encouragement to those who would listen. You can take this one step further by factoring in the common belief in guardian angels, suggesting that not only are angels sent to advise, but they are also tasked with protecting a certain individual from harm whenever possible.

Fortunately, you don't have to subscribe to a particular religion in order to discover and communicate with your spirit guide. Such guides exist no matter what your belief system is. Even atheists have spirit guides assigned to them, meaning that you don't have to earn their help; you simply have to accept it. Furthermore, spirit guides can take many different shapes and forms, each possessing unique qualities and benefits that are usually tailored for the individual they serve. The following are some of the most common forms of spirit guides, along with the basic nature of their role in your life:

- **Angels:** As mentioned, angels are the messengers of the spirit realm. Often seen in terms of the counterpart to demons, they can advise you to choose the right path when temptation entices you to choose the wrong path—one that will prove dangerous and ultimately disastrous. Archangels are the highest form of angels, considered the most proficient and powerful. Some archangels are fairly well known through stories and traditions, including Michael, Gabriel, and Rafael. If you are lucky enough to be in contact with an archangel, you can be assured that your future is very promising indeed!
- **Ancestors:** Another common tradition held throughout the world and human history is the idea that deceased relatives can play a role in guiding and protecting their loved ones in this life. This is particularly true in the case of departed parents or grandparents, people who had a very close and vested interest in you while they were still alive. The belief here is that their love keeps them close to you for a while, enabling them to send encouragement and love in times of distress or general loneliness.
- **Spirit Animals:** Almost everyone has heard the term "totem animal" used in one context or another. Unfortunately, most people have only experienced totem animals in terms of online quizzes that are for entertainment purposes only. The truth is that spirit animals serve a much greater purpose than merely fodder for party conversations. They can give you the elemental strength and courage you need to face even the most daunting of challenges, bringing out your best "nature" when you need it the most.
- **Deities:** Ancient societies worshipped many gods and goddesses, something not commonly done in modern times. One of the reasons for this is that it allowed the ancients to contemplate the various aspects of humanity. Zeus, for example, could serve to embody leadership, fatherly love, and the wisdom of an older person. Aphrodite, in contrast,

represented physical beauty and carnal pleasure. Thus, each deity could appear to the individual in order to reinforce certain elements of that person's character. If you start seeing visions of gods or goddesses, rather than being a construct of your imagination, it could be a real message—one providing you with the answers you need.

- **Religious Figures:** Many people around the world have claimed to have seen visions or heard messages from Jesus, Mary, the Buddha, and other such religious figures. While some of these claims may be hoaxes, many are probably the real deal, suggesting that the spirits of these once corporeal souls are still trying to influence people, leading them along the right path when times are tough and hard choices need to be made.

- **Sacred Figures:** Almost all spiritual traditions have sacred figures of one form or another. Priests, shamans, popes, elders, and wisdom women help lead the practitioners of their tradition while on Earth. What many don't realize is that they continue to serve in this capacity even when departed. It is as though their soul continues to fulfill their calling despite their body being long gone. Having a sacred figure as a spirit guide is not only a gift beyond measure; it is a chance for you to access all of the knowledge that guides spend a lifetime discovering.

How to Detect your Spirit Guides

Now that you have an idea as to the different types of spirit guides and the forms they take, the next step is to detect the spirit guide or guides that are trying to help you live the best life possible. This is where your psychic abilities will prove themselves more useful than ever. The bottom line is that spirit guides are just that— spirits. Therefore, you can't expect to see, hear, or experience them with your physical senses—at least not at first. Instead, you have to tap into your psychic senses, your clairs, and use them to detect your spirit guides with your inner eye, inner ear, or whatever inner sense is strongest for you.

Not surprisingly, dreams are an ideal way to detect your spirit guides. This is because dreams are nothing but internal, meaning your inner senses are at their highest level since your physical senses are quite literally asleep. There are two ways in which your dreams can reveal the identity of your spirit guides. First, try to recall your dreams from the past, especially when you were struggling with difficult issues in the waking world. Did you dream of a religious figure coming to offer you encouragement or support? Perhaps a dream character shows up regularly, especially when you are struggling the most. Or have specific animals been in your dreams, awakening your primal energies for the challenges at hand? If you have had any such dreams, recognize them as nothing less than an encounter with your spirit guide. Needless to say, write these dreams down immediately, much the way you would the name and phone number of someone you just met.

The second way dreams can help detect your spirit guide is through the process of dream incubation. This is where you spend time just before going to sleep telling yourself to have dreams of a specific sort. For example, if you wanted to dream about being rich and famous, you would meditate on the specifics before falling asleep, creating the dream environment for you to realize your fantasies. This same process can be used to discover the identity of your spirit guides. In this case, take the time before falling asleep to meditate on a particular place, like a café or a park bench. Imagine your spirit guide meeting you there. They may already be there, or they may come and find you. In any event, when you find yourself on that park bench, don't dismiss the first person who sits next to you as they are probably your spirit guide.

Synchronicity is another common way in which spirit guides can send messages. Therefore, if you want to know who your spirit guide is, ask for a pattern to emerge in your waking life. For example, if you see numerous images of angels throughout your day, including pictures, statues, and other forms, then take that as the answer. If you see images of a particular deity or the name of a deity, then don't dismiss that as coincidence. Animals can also present themselves—although don't imagine that your totem animal is a squirrel if you spend the day in a park where squirrels are a dime a dozen. What you are looking for are signs that are out of the ordinary. If you see images of lions all day long, then that might be the answer you seek. But don't go to the zoo looking for inspiration.

If you are faced with information overload and don't know whether you are seeing a pattern or mere coincidence, there are two things you can do to solve the confusion. First, take a couple of days off and try again later when your mind is open and your heart ready. When you see the same signs or images repeat, then you have your answer. The second thing is to turn to your gut feeling. Although the signs are physical, the message is still psychic in nature; therefore, you should feel it as well as see it. If the pattern resonates within your soul, then you know you have your answer. However, if you don't feel a connection or a good feeling about what you are observing, then it is probably just a fluke, and you can ignore it, looking elsewhere for your sign to appear.

How to Communicate with your Spirit Guides

When it comes to communicating with your spirit guides, the best approach is to treat it as though you are developing a relationship with them. When you strip away the details, such as the nature of your spirit guides or the role they play in your life, what you are left with is the dynamic of creating a strong, caring and even loving relationship. Therefore, treat the process of creating a relationship with your spirit guides the same way that you would if you were creating a relationship with a significant other. The first step is to talk to them regularly. Even if you don't hear them respond at first, talk to them as much as you can. Don't just turn to them for help in your time of need. Chat with them daily. Tell them how happy you are that they are there. Ask them how their day is. Even though this may seem ridiculous, at first, the more you talk to your guides, the stronger your connection will become. This means that you will hear them better when you need to call on them for help, so it is not just about having fun; it's also about developing certain vital skill sets.

The next step is to take the time to listen. You might choose to meditate to tune in to your spirit guides, or you might simply pause after you ask a question or make a statement in order to hear the message they have in response. This is a good opportunity to discover how your spirit guides choose to communicate with you. If you are skilled with clairaudience, then the chances are that they will choose to speak to you, so you must take the time to sit in a quiet place and listen for their voice. Alternatively, they may be the sort of spirits that use signs to get their message across. If, for example, you want to know the name of your guardian angel, then after you ask the question, take the time to listen. If you hear a name pop into your head, go with it, even if it's disappointing, at first. Not everyone can have Archangel Michael as their guide. Yours might, in fact, be Bob or Sue. Don't be snobbish and dismiss the name, waiting for something better.

However, if you don't hear a name, start looking for one. Look for names on billboards, TV ads, restaurant signs, and the like. Don't go through the phonebook looking for the name that sounds right; let the name come to you. That is the point of listening, after all. Have faith that your spirit guide is capable enough to get a message across to you if you put in the effort to try and hear what they have to say. Using synchronicity is a good way to confirm the name you heard in your head in the event you had an audio response. For example, if you heard the name Rose, then take the time to look for confirmation throughout the day. Ask for signs to confirm the message. You never know, you might receive a bouquet of roses out of the blue, telling you that you heard the name of your spirit guide loud and clear. This may seem farfetched, and even silly to the newcomer, but anyone with experience in communicating with spirit guides will tell you that they often love to use humor, making you smile while conveying the message you need to hear. In fact, you can think of it as them showing off their skills, or rewarding you for your efforts by treating you to something meaningful and fun.

This method of asking and listening is the same method you will use whether you ask your spirit guides for their name or for guidance on making an important decision at hand. However, when it comes to issues that have a "yes or no" quality to them, you can fall back on gut feeling. You don't need to spend the day listening for a voice to say yes or no, nor do you need to look for the first answer that presents itself in plain sight. Instead, listen to your heart. This is where your psychic communication takes place anyway. Therefore, if someone offers you a job, for example, clear your mind, ask your guides whether this is the right move, and then feel the answer. If you feel uplifted, even euphoric, then that is them telling you to go for it. Alternatively, if you feel anxious or even a sense of dread, then graciously decline the offer, knowing that your guides have spared you future hardship and pain.

Ways to Develop your Ability to Communicate with your Spirit Guides

The final thing you will want to do is to strengthen your ability to communicate with your spirit guides. Again, one of the best ways to achieve this goal is to practice every day, just like you would when trying to improve any other psychic ability or any ability at all for that matter. The more you practice, the better you will get; it's really that simple. Therefore, start by talking and listening to your guides, asking simple and basic questions, at first, such as what form they take and what they wish to be called. The more time and effort you spend asking the easy questions, the better prepared you will be when it comes to tackling the more important issues.

The next thing you need to do is keep a journal. This is a critical practice in developing any psychic skill set. In this case, you will want to record all of the messages you receive. Write down the message itself, such as a name or an answer to a question. Then write down the form the message took. Did you hear it, see it or dream it? No matter how it came to you, write it down. Finally, write down whether the message proved to be true or not. In the beginning, you will find that many of the messages you hear are products of your thoughts and imagination. It takes time to sort out the voices of your guides from the other thoughts and ideas in your head. That is why you want to keep a journal. Eventually, a pattern will develop, one that shows the method by which you have had the most success. For example, if your dreams prove spot on every time, then focus on your dreams as your primary source of communication. Research dream dynamics and do everything you can to be the best when it comes to creating, experiencing, and recalling your dreams. If the answers you hear are the ones that prove more accurate, then take the time and effort to develop clairaudience. In the end, use your journal as a learning tool, one that will show you what works best and what doesn't. You can also use your journal to help keep track of ways to develop your skills once you have discovered your spirit guides' chosen form of communication.

Finally, ask for help. As with any relationship, both parties need to be on the same page. If you want to know how your spirit guides choose to communicate, ask them. This should be one of the first questions you ask—if not the absolute first. After all, only when you know how to find the answers will it make sense to ask any other questions. Once you know the form of communication your guides prefer, you can ask them what you need to do in order to improve your ability to communicate with them. You might find an advertisement on TV that provides inspiration, or a billboard might have a statement that hits home. In the end, your spirit guides are there to help you succeed, so they won't make it difficult. All you need to do is be patient with yourself, allowing yourself time to learn while not getting frustrated at the mistakes you make. Always keep an open mind and never give up. Developing a relationship with spirits won't always be easy, even if it is your personal psychic gift. However, the rewards that such a relationship can provide will be beyond measure, making the time and effort more worthwhile than you can possibly imagine. Once you develop a rich and meaningful relationship with your spirit guides, you will never again have to face another day alone. And that in and of itself can be enough to change your life completely, enabling you to live the happy, loving, and fulfilling life you both desire and deserve.

Conclusion

Now that you have read this book, you have all the tools you need to identify and develop your personal psychic abilities. Whether you are a natural-born healer, a clairvoyant, or a medium able to channel messages from departed souls, you can begin to hone your skills so that you can use your abilities to live a life of untold wonder and purpose. Furthermore, by following the instructions on meditation and general practices for improving mental and physical wellbeing, you will improve your life on every level. This will help reduce your stress, improve your energy levels, and provide you with the peace of mind you truly deserve. Finally, once you develop the ability to clear your mind of the clutter of day-to-day life, you will be able to tap into the spirit realm in ways you never imagined possible. Whether it's seeing events before they unfold, hearing the thoughts of a loved one miles away, or even speaking to spirit guides, you will discover abilities and talents that transcend physical reality, taking your life experience to a whole new dimension. The very best of luck to you as you embark on your journey of exploring and developing your psychic abilities.

Your Free Gift (only available for a limited time)

Thanks for getting this book! If you want to learn more about various spirituality topics, then join Mari Silva's community and get a free guided meditation MP3 for awakening your third eye. This guided meditation mp3 is designed to open and strengthen ones third eye so you can experience a higher state of consciousness. Simply visit the link below the image to get started.

https://spiritualityspot.com/meditation

References

Third Eye Science – Psychology Today

https://www.psychologytoday.com/us/blog/stuck/200908/third-eye-science

The Third Eye

https://www.ukessays.com/essays/philosophy/the-third-eye-philosophy-essay.php

https://somuchyoga.com/what-are-chakras/

https://lonerwolf.com/how-to-open-your-third-eye/

https://yogainternational.com/article/view/what-are-the-7-chakras

https://www.chakras.info/what-is-chakra/

https://www.the-energy-healing-site.com/chakra-blockages.html

https://www.color-meanings.com/chakra-colors-the-7-chakras-and-their-meanings/

https://blog.sivanaspirit.com/sp-gn-imbalanced-chakras-remedies/

https://blog.mindvalley.com/symptoms-of-blocked-chakras/

https://naturalchakrahealing.com/elements.html

https://tantricacademy.com/history-of-the-chakras/

https://psy-minds.com/the-third-eye-2/

https://www.templepurohit.com/the-third-eye-of-lord-shiva-significance-symbolism/

https://www.mumblesandthings.com/blog/2017/4/17/how-to-tell-if-your-third-eye-chakra-is-blocked

https://www.chakras.info/third-eye-chakra/

https://www.gaia.com/article/pineal-third-eye-chakra

http://psychic-energy-healing.com/third-eye-opening/herbs-to-decalcify-the-pineal-gland-and-open-the-third-eye/

https://humanoriginproject.com/ways-to-heal-pineal-gland-calcification-open-the-third-eye/

https://www.tokenrock.com/explain-pineal-gland-73.html

https://www.endocrineweb.com/endocrinology/overview-pineal-gland

https://www.healthline.com/health/pineal-gland-function

https://www.chakras.info/opening-third-eye/

https://intuitivejourney.com/third-eye-opening-exercises/

https://intuitivesoulsblog.com/third-eye/

https://www.pinterest.com/moorevision/central-and-peripheral-vision/

https://innerouterpeace.com/third-eye-opening-symptoms/

https://www.headspace.com/meditation-101/what-is-meditation

https://www.meditationiseasy.com/meditation-techniques/trataka-the-meditation-technique-of-third-eye/

https://heartofsubstance.com/meditation-for-intuition/

https://www.jonathanparker.org/meditation/third-eye-meditation-open-intuition/

https://www.thedailymeditation.com/how-to-use-the-third-eye-meditation-technique

https://learnrelaxationtechniques.com/chakra-meditations-for-beginners/

https://www.the-guided-meditation-site.com/mindfulness-exercises.html

https://www.chakraboosters.com/best-third-eye-chakra-foods

https://www.naturmend.com/blog/2019/01/28/nourishing-your-third-eye-chakra/

https://www.allchakras.com/third-eye-chakra-affirmations/

https://psychicelements.com/blog/psychic-dreams/

https://www.beliefnet.com/wellness/2009/06/9-things-you-need-to-know-about-psychic-premonition.aspx

https://articles.spiritsciencecentral.com/third-eye-crystals/

http://www.chakrabalance.org/what-to-expect

https://psychiclibrary.com/aura-colors-and-meanings/

https://bodysoulmind.net/soul/your-aura

https://www.speakingtree.in/allslides/the-scientific-evidence-of-human-aura

https://www.7chakracolors.com/blog/see-aura-illustrated-exercises/

https://in5d.com/how-to-read-auras-what-is-the-meaning-of-each-color/

https://www.psychics4today.com/signs-of-clairvoyance/

https://www.psychics4today.com/how-to-develop-psychic-abilities/

https://uk.iacworld.org/how-to-exercise-your-psychic-abilities-the-iac-approach/

https://keleger.com/gods-mercy/the-third-eye-spiritual-gifts/

https://psychicelements.com/blog/psychic-abilities/

https://www.keen.com/articles/psychic/psychic-intuitive-medium-whats-the-difference

https://www.aetherius.org.nz/develop-intuition-psychic-abilities/

https://www.amazon.com/Psychic-Development-Beginners-Naturally-Intuition-ebook/dp/B00YCBT838/ref=sr_1_5?keywords=psychic+development+for+beginners&qid=1572852362&sr=8-5

https://www.psychicgurus.org/5-fun-activities-for-psychic-development/

https://intuitivesoulsblog.com/develop-your-psychic-abilities/

https://www.psychicgurus.org/psychic-meditation/

https://www.psychicperformer.com/4-spiritual-practices-that-can-improve-your-psychic-connection/

https://www.amazon.com/Discover-Your-Psychic-Type-Developing/dp/0738712787/ref=sr_1_6?crid=136JF0LCTW3AN&keywords=developing+psychic+abilities&qid=1572989803&s=books&sprefix=developing+psychic+%2Caps%2C435&sr=1-6

https://www.annasayce.com/which-is-your-strongest-intuitive-gift/

https://www.psychologytoday.com/us/blog/debunking-myths-the-mind/201804/the-biology-telepathy

https://www.psychicgurus.org/how-to-read-minds-telepathically/

https://www.oprah.com/spirit/what-is-a-medium-rebecca-rosen

https://www.amandalinettemeder.com/blog/2014/12/23/7-steps-to-improve-your-mediumship-abilities

https://www.psychicgurus.org/psychometry/

https://www.gaia.com/article/how-to-see-auras

https://www.psychicgurus.org/psychic-healing/

https://www.psychokinesispowers.com/psychic-healing-techniques

https://www.ncbi.nlm.nih.gov/pmc/articles/PMC4107996/

https://intuitivesoulsblog.com/psychic-development-tip-2-meet-spirit-guides/

https://www.erinpavlina.com/blog/2006/11/connecting-with-spirit-guides/

https://www.huffpost.com/entry/encounters-with-psychics_n_56c4c530e4b0b40245c8b5b1

https://liveanddare.com/types-of-meditation/

https://www.annasayce.com/the-forgotten-clairs-clairgustance-and-clairsalience/

https://www.huffpost.com/entry/the-habits-of-highly-intu_n_4958778

https://www.heysigmund.com/9-ways-to-tap-into-your-intuition-and-why-youll-want-to/

https://www.bustle.com/p/11-ways-to-know-if-your-intuition-is-trying-to-tell-you-something-how-to-listen-38787

https://www.poweredbyintuition.com/2013/04/28/13-examples-of-intuition-in-everyday-life-from-top-creatives/

http://beyondiam.com/examples-of-intuition/

https://consciouslifenews.com/7-easy-ways-develop-telepathic-abilities/11103458/#

https://www.headspace.com/meditation/techniques

https://forums.forteana.org/index.php?threads/smoke-billets-pictures-from-the-other-side.52237/

https://www.amandalinettemeder.com/blog/the-4-main-types-of-mediumship

https://www.psychologytoday.com/us/blog/neuronarrative/201212/study-finds-the-unexpected-in-the-brains-spirit-mediums-0

https://www.color-meanings.com/spiritual-colors-the-difference-between-auras-and-chakras/

https://aura.net/chakras-auras-work-together/

https://www.psychics4today.com/how-to-see-auras/

https://www.gaia.com/article/what-is-a-spirit-guide

https://www.speakingtree.in/allslides/the-scientific-evidence-of-human-aura

https://gostica.com/aura-science/layers-of-the-aura/#:~:targetText=Energy%20body%20(or%20aura)%20has,and%20the%20immediate%20external%20environment.&targetText=Each%20layer%20or%20level%20is%20an%20energy%20field%20varying%20in%20vibration.

Printed in Great Britain
by Amazon